CW00434964

Steve:
unwanted

Steve: unwanted

STEVE WALKER

First published in 2011 by Short Books
3a Exmouth House
Pine Street
EC1R 0JH
1 2 3 4 5 6 7 8 9 10

This paperback edition published in 2012

Copyright ©
Steve Walker 2011

Steve Walker has asserted his right under the Copyright,
Designs and Patents Act 1988 to be identified as the author of
this work. All rights reserved. No part of this publication
may be reproduced, stored in a retrieval system or transmitted in
any form, or by any means (electronic, mechanical, or
otherwise) without the prior written permission of both
the copyright owners and the publisher.

A CIP catalogue record for this book
is available from the British Library.

Jacket image: Niall McDiarmid/Millenium Images, UK

ISBN 978-1-78072-041-8

Printed and bound by CPI Group (UK) Ltd, Croydon, CR0 4YY

Contents

CHAPTER 1

Childhood

I was born in 1950 at Brook Street Hospital and grew up in Lambeth, south London. My mother abandoned me on my grandparents' doorstep when I was just eleven months old, so I have no memories of her whatsoever. I don't even have a photograph, so I have no idea what she looked like, or whether I resemble her in any way. I've never met her since – I don't even know if she is still alive – so I don't know for sure why caring for a child was too much for her nor why she took the drastic step that she did.

I've been told that her name was Doreen Parker. I don't know what age Doreen was when she married my father, or what age she was when I was born. She just disappeared into the ether and, so far as my family told me, was never seen again.

My father and grandparents often told me that Doreen had been a "lady of the night", a prostitute, and I don't know whether this was true or not. They were hardly likely to be kind and impartial under the circumstances; having raised eleven children of their own, Nan and Grandad were starting all over again with me at a stage in their lives when they might reasonably have expected to be able to start taking things a little more easily.

I like to think that in choosing my grandparents to look after her baby boy, Doreen was doing the best she could in what must have been very difficult circumstances for her. No doubt she had her reasons for not keeping me or leaving me with my father, and I hope that they were good ones.

As a child, I did my best to ignore or block out any comments I heard about my mother, because they hurt more than I ever admitted. For years, I thought that I hadn't paid much attention to them, but looking back now, I believe that being told such awful things about my biological mother every time her name came up caused serious emotional problems for me later on.

Many children who grow up without a parent develop fantasies about how, one day, they will come back and find them. But I never did. I was never allowed to talk about my mother; it was a taboo subject. I just tried to get on with each day as it came and I hardly ever wondered about Doreen Parker. I have never found out what happened to her. For all I know, she is still living, and I presume that I may have uncles and aunts and siblings somewhere out there. At this stage, I just have to accept that I will never know.

I grew up as an only child with Nan and Grandad. My father was not around very much, even though he lived quite close by. We lived in Hutton Road in a small two-up, two-down house like so many others in the city. I slept in the same room as my grandparents because my uncle Albie, a single man, used the other bedroom. Uncle Albie was, at about fifteen years older than me, the youngest of Nan and Grandad's many children.

I didn't have a bed. I had to sleep on a rather lumpy, old-fashioned settee, from which I could see through a hatch out onto the stairway. This view regularly frightened the life out of me because of all the noises and sounds I could hear in the house and because of the shadows that I would often see dancing against the wall. I frequently had vivid nightmares and would sleepwalk. On one occasion, Uncle Albie stopped me from climbing out of the bedroom window, which was much closer to the floor than would be the case in a modern house. I don't remember what any of my nightmares were about.

My grandparents were good people and they did their best for me. But it wasn't easy for them to play the role of mum and dad at their age, even with Uncle Albie's help – especially because my real father, Reg, was a difficult man who wasn't willing or able to help out on anything like a regular basis. Dad was a very heavy drinker; an alcoholic, in fact. He had a good job as a steel erector, but went through the money he earned very quickly. He loved to gamble and regularly lost all of his money down at the bookies' where, despite all the evidence to the contrary, he was always sure he would make his fortune one day.

Dad had serious problems with his temper, too. He used to call round Nan's occasionally for Sunday lunch, or to sort me out when I had played up, especially as I grew older and more difficult to deal with. He would come round, threaten me by saying that I should behave or else, or give me a good hiding and tell me that Nan and Grandad didn't want me and were going to put me in a children's home, so they could be rid of me and all my annoying ways.

I was afraid of my father, and I think that my grandparents were often afraid of him, too. He didn't seem to have a great deal of control over his emotions and was liable to lash out like a man possessed when things weren't to his liking. And things often weren't to his liking. I remember one Sunday when he came round straight from the pub, and complained that the dinner Nan had prepared was cold. When this wasn't dealt with quickly enough for him, Dad started screaming and shouting his complaints, telling Nan that she was bloody useless and that the least he should expect after the hard week that he had had was a good, hot dinner. The tantrum climaxed when he smashed his plate over Nan's head.

"Call that a Sunday dinner?" he screamed. "I wouldn't fucking give that to a dog. It's like something you'd find beside a lamp-post. That's not food; I don't want it." He stamped off in a rage, slamming the door so hard behind him that the glass in the front window shook.

I remember Nan just standing there with gravy and blood pouring down her face. There was so much blood it half-filled the old enamel pail that she always used to wash the floor. Her head had been split wide open, and she had to go to hospital for treatment. I remember Grandad trying to stop the flow of blood as best he could while we waited for the ambulance to come.

I was hysterical and frightened, wondering whether Nan was going to die and what would happen to me if she did. I cried and cried but wanted to stay with her while she was being looked after. Eventually, Auntie Pat from across the road, Dad's older sister, came to collect me, to look after me, as the ambulance arrived to take my grandmother away.

Nan was only in her fifties at that time, but she looked a lot older in her hospital bed when I was taken to visit her. I don't know if my father ever apologised for what he had done, but he was back again not long after that and everything was back to what passed for normal for him, so I suppose Nan must have decided to forgive and forget – or that it was easier to carry on as though nothing had happened. I accepted that this was just the way it was. There was nothing anybody could do about my father's behaviour, so we just worked around it as best we could.

On other occasions, Dad would be told about some misdemeanour or other that I had committed, and he would teach me a lesson the only way he knew how: he would give me a good thump and issue some more recriminations and threats. Having seen what he had done to Nan, I was sure that he meant them.

Reg was very much the black sheep of the family; the rest of his brothers and sisters had done quite well in life and most of them had settled down, had children of their own, and just got on with things. Dad was the third oldest of the eleven children in his family. Everyone told me that he had been a tearaway from the start, that Nan and Grandad had always had their work cut out with him, and that the teachers had found him impossible, too.

When he was a boy, our street was still lit by gas lamps, and one of my dad's favourite tricks was to climb up them to get a light for his fag and to put out the gas light while he was there. He often told me this story, and thought it was hilarious. Throughout his childhood and adolescence, his parents had regularly had to deal with the police knocking on their door about some trouble or other that he had been up to. I think he must have had a hard time growing up, and presume that Grandad had been tough on him, the way he was tough on me. But because my father and I never talked very much, I can only guess at the details of what went on between them. My feeling is that he was a very unhappy man all the time I knew him, because his behaviour was not that of a person at peace with himself and the world.

Unfortunately, as I got older, it became obvious from the way I behaved and interacted with others that I had learned a lot from my dad, although thankfully, at this stage I was never violent towards Nan and Grandad. I shared my dad's short temper and tendency to fly off the handle when things didn't go well for me. I also found it very difficult to articulate my feelings and tell people that I needed some support when things weren't going well for me.

Like my father, when I had a problem I kept it to myself for as long as I could and tried to pretend that it wasn't there and that I had the situation under control, although I almost never did. Eventually, the problem would escalate and I would explode in a fit of rage and shame. These tendencies would cause me a lot of problems at school and later on.

When I was six I was sent to the local school – Vauxhall Primary School – a few roads from where I lived. It was an ordinary school in most respects, but the playground was on the roof, about four floors up.

From as far back as I can remember, I was the dunce of the class. I found schoolwork impossibly difficult, didn't know when or how to ask for help and had a lot of problems dealing with the teachers and all their demands. All the other children mastered reading and writing, but I would just stare miserably at the page with a complete lack of comprehension. I was a bit better at maths, but not enough to make up for my shortcomings in the area of literacy.

The school, on Vauxhall Street in Lambeth, was quite rough, and any child who stood out as being different was a natural target for bullies. All the other children in the class seemed to be brighter than me by a long shot. They could all read quite well, while I was still struggling to spell out my name. They used to take the mickey out of me because I was stupid, and also because I didn't have a mum or a proper dad and was one of the poorest children in the class; the one with the tatty clothes and the snotty face.

"What's the matter with you, Steve?" one kid would ask. "Did your mum drop you on your head or something?"

"He doesn't even *have* a mum!" someone else would say gleefully. "And he doesn't have a proper dad, either."

"Yeah, probably because they didn't want him, eh? Nobody wanted you, did they, Steve?"

So I couldn't read, and I couldn't write, and on top of that I never had any new clothes. I wore hand-me-downs that Nan had picked up from my aunts and uncles. I was small for my age, too, a bit of a runt, and so naturally I became the whipping boy for the whole class.

I hated going to school, because every day I felt as though I had been picked out for special torture at the hands of the other kids. Since then, I have always been very sympathetic towards kids who are being bullied, as I know exactly what it feels like and how powerless the victim is. Things may be better in schools now, but in those days there was little or no support for the child who was struggling and being bullied. The general attitude seemed to be that if you didn't stand up for yourself, you more or less deserved what you got. School was supposed to toughen kids up, and getting bullied was part of the educational process. Because the school was big and the classes were large, it was run along military lines. As a matter of fact, I believe that a lot of the teachers had army backgrounds. This was the 1950s, so a lot of the men would have been in the Second World War as young-sters. Believe me, it showed.

Teaching in my school was very much an exercise in crowd control. The teachers would yell out orders in the large classrooms – and you'd be in for it if you didn't do what you were told! One of the teachers was very much like a sergeant major. His way of teaching English was to get each child up in front of the class to read from a book, whether they could manage it or not. I couldn't. I was painfully shy, and I wasn't just slow to pick up reading and writing; I remained almost completely illiterate throughout my education.

I can still remember standing in front of the class and looking at the book, unable to decipher even a single word. The words were just like black scratches on the page and they conveyed no meaning to me whatsoever. After a while, the teacher screamed at me to sit down and stop wasting everybody's time, and the rest of the children sniggered "stupid bastard!" as

I made my way back towards my seat, trying not to cry and wiping my snotty nose on my sleeve. I was often made to look stupid because I couldn't read, and I was often made to stand in the corner facing the wall, the better to think about my shortcomings and what I needed to do about them. This made me feel really angry; it wasn't my fault that I couldn't read and it felt like nobody was trying to help. Most of the teachers gave up on me. The children just laughed at me. Nan and Grandad were in no position to help.

Children who failed to do what they were supposed to be able to manage were sent to the headmistress to be punished. Needless to say, I spent a lot of time shuffling down the long corridor towards her office, waiting to hear the riot act yet again. With each year that passed, I became more conscious of all the things I didn't have and couldn't do. I learned that my illiteracy was something to be embarrassed about and ashamed of.

The school system offered free dinners to children from poor families, and of course I was eligible. This was a good system insofar as it ensured that everyone had at least one square meal a day. But children being children, it was used as a way to single out the weak ones and make fun of them. The teachers dealt with it quite insensitively. They would shout out, "Hey, Steve, are you having free milk today? Are you down for a free dinner?" and I would feel as though all eyes were upon me. If there was a school trip, the expense of bringing me was subsidised by the school and everybody knew about that, as well. I was sure that all the other children were talking about me and saying things like, "That's Steve. The school has to give him free dinners and pay for his school trip because he has no mum and dad and his grandparents are poor."

On those rare days when I brought in homemade sandwiches and rolls, or a little pocket money, I could never hold onto them for long because I was small and weak and pathetic and someone would hit me or just threaten to hit me and make off with my lunch or my sixpence. I never told Nan or Grandad about these instances because in those days you were expected to fight your own corner, and you would just get a clip around the ear for not being able to stand up for yourself. It would have been worse to have Nan and Grandad sort my problems out than make do with no sandwiches.

Eventually, I remember, I made a very conscious, very deliberate decision that I was not going to put up with being bullied any longer, and that I was going to start to fight my corner and learn how to stand up for myself at whatever cost. So one day, I found myself face to face with the kid who was known to be the top fighter in the school: Archie.

The very mention of Archie spread tremors of fear all over school. Like me, Archie was about nine years old and a local boy. To an adult, he would probably have looked like any little kid, with tousled hair and a snotty face. To the children he knew, he was a bully and a tyrant and the object of tremendous fear. Archie had few enemies, because nobody was brave enough to stand up to him. I decided that I would risk everything and take him on. One day, Archie took my rolls from me and demanded my pocket money. I decided there and then that I would not give in to him but would stand up and fight him. Even if I lost, at least I would have done my best. I lifted my chin and said, "If you want it, you've got to take it off me."

"Are you fucking joking?" Archie asked in disbelief. "*You* want to fight with *me*?"

"I'll do it," I squeaked. "And I'll win, too."

We started fighting in the school playground and it wasn't long before a crowd gathered to watch all the excitement. I looked into Archie's eyes and saw no fear. But something very strange was happening. Boys who usually looked at me only when I had done something to attract their ridicule were shouting; shouting for *me* to win, not Archie. They didn't like me very much, but they really hated Archie. They spurred me on and, from somewhere, I managed to find the strength to knock Archie to the ground. I sat on top of him, stared into his face and asked him if he wanted any more. Archie surrendered, the crowd cheered and started chanting my name, and I felt like a hero. I had beaten the school bully.

That was a wonderful day and a big awakening for me, because I had learned that I could stand up for myself and give it all I had. I had learned how to fight; I thought I had learned how to be a man. I swaggered home that afternoon, full of bravado and determined never to look back. Never again would I put up with the bullying and the mickey-taking; the name-calling and the sly back-stabbing. From now on, I was going to do whatever it took to stay on the top. And, sure enough, from then on the other kids looked at me differently. I liked to think that it was admiration, but it was probably fear, because now I was the new Archie.

From then on, I ceased to be a bullied little runt and knew I could look after myself. I had found a new way to live; a way without being scared. I wasn't going to let the bastards get me down ever again. I had earned the respect of my peers, if not their friendship, and I was prepared to settle for that. That was good enough for me.

Despite my new-found status, I remember feeling utterly alone throughout my primary school years. I had no real parents, no older siblings to stand up for me and no younger siblings to lord it over at home. I respected my grandparents, but I think I was protective of them, in a way, and didn't want them to know how badly school was going for me. Nan and Grandad doted on me, and although I was often resentful of having to be in earlier than the other children on the street, I loved them both very much. They had a lot of time for me and did the best they could in what were quite difficult circumstances for them.

Money was rather tight and they had to be careful with every penny. Nan worked hard as a cleaner on trains and buses and in stations, and my grandfather wasn't able to work because of an injury he had received to his arm. Years before, he'd had a job for the council. He had always cycled to work. One day, he was on his way to work when he caught the front wheel of his push-bike in a tramline and ended up suffering a horrific injury. The doctors had considered amputating his arm, but he hadn't let them, preferring to have a mangled arm to no arm at all.

Grandad was a house-husband long before the term was coined, and he was very good at it. He did all the cooking and cleaning, and the house was always spotless from top to bottom. He was so house-proud that I was never allowed to leave my toys around the house, creating clutter and mess. I had to play with them at the table and put them back at the end of the day. I had a Meccano set that I loved and a construction kit that I used to make reconstructions of buildings like Tower Bridge, which moved around and did things when you pressed the right buttons. I had a knack for anything mechanical and could count on Uncle Albie for help, when he was around. Uncle Albie was always very good to me.

Because Nan was out working, Grandad was the one who took care of me after school and made sure that I did my homework and had my bath in a tin tub that was brought inside. I wasn't really able to do my homework, and I don't know if Grandad would have been in a position to help; in any case, he never did. We both just went through the motions.

As my grandparents had had such a large family of their own, there were uncles, aunts and cousins in abundance, and lots of houses where I was welcome for a cup of tea and a slice of bread and butter. Uncle Albie, having no children of his own as yet, was often available. Albie worked as a lorry driver, often driving tipper lorries, which were enormously exciting to a little boy. Some days, when I was off school, Uncle Albie would say, "Steve, mate, do you want to come and help me at work today?" and my heart would swell with pride. "Helping" consisted mostly of sitting beside Uncle Albie and watching what he did, but once in a while, if we were going down a quiet country road to a tip with a load of rubbish, he would let me steer and then, when we got to the dump, even manipulate the levers so that the truck would drop its load. I was in heaven on those days, and when Uncle Albie took me out for a spin on the back of the motorbike.

Everyone was happy when Uncle Albie met a nice girl called Janet and they started courting, but although I liked Janet, I was a bit ambivalent about their relationship. With a pretty girlfriend on the scene, Uncle Albie had less time to take me to the dump, and that was a big loss.

My various aunts helped out with the clothes and toys that their children didn't need any more, as the expense of raising a boy was a lot for my grandparents to deal with at their time of life. My auntie Marge lived right across the street in Hutton Road. I spent a lot of time in her house, and she was always very kind to me. Auntie Pat, who also lived nearby with her husband, Uncle Pip, had three children, my cousins David, Tommy and Jeanie. They were the closest thing I had to sisters and brothers and, while we squabbled at times, we were also quite close.

Auntie Pat's house was a home from home for me. I used to take my bath there sometimes, and she and Uncle Pip generally did their best to treat me like one of their own in every way that they could. They were generous and kind to a fault. If they were taking their children on a day out to the zoo, I would go too. If there were iced buns to go round, there was always one for me. I often stayed the night and got to pretend that I was really at home with a mum and dad who would tuck me in and kiss me goodnight.

I visited other aunts and uncles but remember how confusing I found it to have to juggle the different sets of rules and regulations that went with each household unit. I had to be one person when I was with Auntie Pat and someone else when I was with Uncle Tommy or Auntie Marge, and it was all quite confusing – especially because none of those rules applied when I was at home with Nan and Grandad, but different ones instead.

As well as Uncle Albie, Auntie Pat played a big role in helping to bring me up, partly because of her natural kindness and generosity, and partly because she lived so close by. I also used to visit Uncle Tommy, who lived in Clapham. While he was very good to me, I was a little wary of him because his rules and regulations always struck me as quite rigid. Uncle Tommy had twin girls who were being very carefully brought up, and when I was around he wanted me to be on my best behaviour too. I did my best, but wasn't always able to step up to the mark.

Uncle Tommy taught me to play chess, and to my surprise I was very good at it. He was a good teacher and a good player himself, and liked to enter competitions. I respected him because he never let me win; he taught me how to play and then made sure that I did it properly. I loved being able to think about my next move and work out my strategy, and the fact that Uncle Tommy usually won made my victories all the sweeter.

None of my aunts and uncles ever mentioned Dad. Along with my mother, he was a taboo subject for them. I think they'd all had enough of him and his violent, unpredictable ways.

I do remember having fun with my mates in the street where I lived as a child. On one occasion, a few friends and I made a cart out of old pieces of wood that we had found and great big ball-bearings that we fitted onto wooden axles. We decorated our fine chariot with lots of beer bottle tops – bottle tops were considered very valuable by children at the time. We had a great laugh racing up and down the street, making an incredible amount of noise and annoying the adults, whose irate comments only added to the fun.

Another game we loved to play was called "Knock Down Ginger". This involved tying a dustbin lid to the door knocker of a house. We would then do a "rat-a-tat-tat" on the door, run like hell and hide, peeping out to see what would happen. When the door opened, the dustbin lid would be pulled off, possibly taking the dustbin with it, and we would jump up from our hiding places and run away, laughing like hyenas. We got caught once in a while and ended up with a good clump around the ear, but it didn't put us off.

Uncle Albie finally moved out when I was eleven. He moved into a house around the corner with his girlfriend, Janet, and they planned to get married. Although Uncle Albie obviously had less time for me now, he was still fond of me and still did what he could to help me out.

I can't claim not to have received the attention I needed as a child, because in fact there were many adults in my life. Still, it was difficult to know that I didn't have my own mum and dad to care for me the way I saw my cousins being looked after, to know that I had been left with my grandparents because nobody had really wanted me.

I was grateful to them, but as I got older, I started to rebel more and more against what I saw as their strictness. I started to push the boundaries as far as I could, until Nan and Grandad were forced to resort to summoning Dad with ever-greater frequency, to sort me out and show me who was boss. Dad used to cause havoc every time he came, and his advice or discipline often made things even worse. I remember a particular day when I had got into an argument with another little boy called Paul, who was my best friend at the time. Paul lived on the same street and for as long as I could remember we had played together, sharing toys and gobstoppers. We occasionally fell out, but it never lasted for too long.

This time, it was just one of those silly, children's things. Paul was with his cousin, and they both ganged up on me and told me that I was wrong about whatever it was and that they were right. It was nothing, absolutely nothing; just a little spat of the sort that children have all the time. I ended up crying and went home in tears because I hated the fact that I'd had a falling-out with my best mate. I didn't know that Dad was going to be there. Well, he went livid when he saw me crying, as though it was some sort of an insult to his manhood.

"What the hell is the matter with you?" Dad said. "What are you snivelling about? You look disgusting. Why are you crying?"

"I've been fighting with my best friend," I sniffed. "Paul and Joe said that I was wrong. But I wasn't wrong; I was right."

"Look, you know what you want? You want to stop being so stupid. Look; here's a stick. Take it. *Take* the bloody stick! Now, I'll come down the road with you and if you don't hit him with the stick, I'll hit *you* with it! You've got to learn how to stand up for yourself, haven't you?"

I took the stick. I hit Paul. I hurt him. I made my dad proud. But I knew it was wrong. I just hoped Paul knew that it wasn't really me hitting him, but my dad.

Chapter 2

Adolescence

As I reached puberty and turned into a bolshy teenager, my previously understanding, loving grandparents started to find me more difficult, and they responded by becoming a lot stricter than they had been before; a case of closing the stable door after the horse has bolted if ever there was one.

I had become reconciled to the idea that I was stupid at school, but there was no way I wanted to be a social failure too, so my main interest at this time was impressing my friends and acquaintances on the street with how tough I was and how I wasn't scared of anybody or anything. Nan and Grandad had given me the best start possible with the resources they had, but they were getting older now and they weren't really equipped to deal with an adolescent, let alone a teenager with major learning difficulties and a big chip on his shoulder. Whereas before I had known that they were always there for me, it seemed to me now that they had changed. And although I know now that they still loved me as much as always, at the time I felt very insecure about their feelings towards me, especially because I understood a bit more about what a normal family was supposed to be like, and how different my situation was. I felt that I was a nuisance and that no doubt my poor performance at school was a bitter disappointment to them.

Grandad, in particular, became much harder on me than he had been before – he became intolerant of me and often came across as aggressive and threatening. Looking back, I am sure that he was doing the best he could. He had already seen one of his sons grow up and go off the rails, and probably thought that a little discipline would help to straighten me out and put me on the right path, before it was too late for me. People might see things differently today, but my grandfather was a man of his generation. As a disabled, older man, my grandfather might also have been a little intimidated at the thought of sharing quarters with an angry adolescent whose behaviour was increasingly unpredictable. Perhaps he felt that he needed to be firm and make a stand before I tried anything on.

I hated the feeling of being restrained and restricted when I tried to do things, and I kicked back whenever and however I could. I felt that my grandparents were very unfair to me. I was never allowed to bring my friends home to play, like other kids were. The other kids were allowed to stay out playing in the street until half past eight at night, but Grandad said I had to be home at seven. That meant that if I came home at eight o'clock – which was still earlier than anyone else – I was in for it. Grandad would be waiting at the door for me to come home and I knew I would either get a good hiding or a real telling-off. Then he would stop me going out the next day to punish me.

Because it was important for me to impress my peers, I often ignored the rules and got into trouble for coming home late. Grandad would shout at me and I would shout back. Over time, the arguments escalated until we were threatening each other, filling the small house with loud, angry voices. Coming home to this after a long day at work was extremely upsetting for my grandmother, but there was very little that she could do about it.

As I continued to go through adolescence, I began to get to know sides of my grandfather that I had never seen before, and to realise that this was probably the sort of treatment my father had had when he was growing up. This was probably why he had become so violent and difficult to deal with. And presumably Grandad had also seen this sort of violence when he was a boy. In later years I would learn a lot about how violence begets violence and how unhealthy cycles of behaviour can be transmitted through the generations until something happens to break the pattern.

At this point, my grandparents moved from London to Carshalton in the suburbs, some distance away. This was a time when the state was redeveloping a lot of the more run-down areas of London, such as Lambeth. They were tearing down old, ramshackle buildings and putting in new ones, and council residents were being offered the chance to move to a new area. There were a lot of ambitious ideas around, about regenerating communities, but in practice, while a lot of people moved, the rougher elements just took their villainy with them. People from our area were offered new homes in Brixton and Carshalton, and Nan and Grandad opted for the latter. This meant a new house, a new school and a new set of friends for me, which was just as well, considering how I had managed at the previous school.

For the first time in my life I had my own bedroom, which felt really good. I could sleep on my own and not have to listen to Nan and Grandad snoring and turning over in bed or – horror of horrors – see their pale, elderly legs swinging over the side of the bed in the morning.

I was worried about starting at a new school, Wellbeck Secondary Modern. It had taken me a lot of effort to build up a reputation as a bruiser in primary school, and I was afraid that once again I would be singled out and bullied, that the other kids would find my weak points and use them to hurt me. Because of this, I decided that I would use the first opportunity I got to establish myself as one of the tough ones and, as soon as I had a chance, that I would take on one of the kingpins and beat him.

The kingpin I chose was Steve, who was very much the local hard nut and a source of great fear to most of the other teenagers at the school. We started fighting on one occasion and I am pleased to say that I beat the crap out of him. The other kids and the teachers soon realised that they had a hard case on their hands. From there on, my reputation seemed to precede me wherever I went. I was deemed to be unruly and uncontrollable. Even the older, bigger school prefects feared me and kept out of my way. This was a situation that suited me very well indeed.

Nan had stopped working by now. Cleaning the buses and trains was hard physical work that was really too much for a woman of her age. She did the odd job here and there, but now Nan and Grandad were living off their pensions, with a little help in the form of the child benefit. While there was always enough to eat, it was a pretty modest existence, and every little extra helped.

By the time I reached the age of thirteen, I realised that it was time that I started to contribute. I was a strong lad and not afraid to break a sweat, so I picked up some work labouring for a building firm, Woodcock Brothers of Wimbledon, in the summer holidays. I was proud to pick up my wage packet and hand it over to my grandmother at the end of the week. I liked the work. It was tough and I didn't have to use my brain too much, which meant that it didn't get tied up in knots the way it did at school. I remember Mr Woodcock saying to me, "You're a good lad, Steve, and I'll have a job for you when you finish school." Was I proud!

At fourteen, I got friendly with an older boy, Brian. Brian lived nearby, and was about three years older than me, so he was practically a grown man in my eyes. We shared a great interest in motorbikes and, being that much older, Brian actually had a bike of his own. I started going round to his place to admire it and to talk about mechanics. We soon became firm friends.

Brian's bike was a gorgeous Royal Enfield, glittering with chrome. I thought it was the happiest day of my life when Brian offered to teach me how to ride it. Although he was from a rather chaotic family too, Brian was quite sensible and worried about me when I got into trouble, something that was happening with increasing frequency. Brian lived with his mum and his brother. I never found out where his dad was – dead, in prison or just disappeared. It was unstated but clear that it just wasn't right to ask. As someone whose dad wasn't on the scene either, I understood the niceties of the situation straight away and never even wondered about him. I had always hated it when people asked where my parents were and I was sensitive enough to realise that Brian was in a similar situation.

Like any teenager, I loved music and wanted to be on top of what was cool at any given moment. It was a hugely exciting day when I got my first record player – a present from Nan and Grandad. It was in what looked like a suitcase; I could open it up, plug it in and play one single at a time. Having a record player made it possible for me to invite mates like Brian round to my place. Adopting a nonchalant air, I'd say, "Alright, mate, want to come round and listen to some music later?" They'd come over and we'd go and sit on my bed and listen to the hits of the day.

The Beatles were big at the time, and Jimi Hendrix. I remember discussing how they got a lot of their ideas from taking drugs and realising that the music and the lyrics were out of this world. As I had never taken drugs, the psychedelic content of the songs didn't mean that much to me. I just knew that this music was much better than the old-fashioned things that Nan and Grandad loved and listened to on the radio and on their own precious gramophone: Bill Haley and Frank Sinatra. I daydreamed about learning how to play the guitar, or maybe the drums, but I never got around to it.

Although I was failing dismally academically, I was good at sports. I could swim very well and even got onto the school diving team. I was good at cricket, too, and held my own at football and basketball. We had great PE instructors in the school, who really pushed us to be as good as we could, and I loved the fact that at least this was one area where I was better than most of the other students.

I think that, if I'd had more help in primary school, I might have done alright, because at Wellbeck I belatedly discovered that I loved history, even if I was not able to read the books or hand in essays, and that I was quite good at maths and woodwork. Interpreting numbers did not seem to cause me the same difficulties as reading did. But I had fallen so far behind that it was too late for me to catch up, and Nan and Grandad were frequently called in to have a word with the headmaster.

In the end, I did as badly at Wellbeck Secondary Modern as I had done before. I regularly got into scraps with the other students, and one day things escalated more than ever before. Involved in a fight in the cloakroom with my classmate, Bob, I completely lost control. I pulled out a lighter that my father had given me and started waving it about. I had started smoking at fourteen or so, to Nan's dismay, but Dad didn't mind. He even encouraged it; it was something that we now had in common. I didn't like the cigarettes at first, but saw them as something that would make me look cool, big and grown-up. They also gave me something to do with my hands when I was feeling awkward. After a while, the taste grew on me, and I became a regular smoker.

In the cloakroom, I flicked the button on the lighter and used the flame to set Bob's hair on fire. I tried to pat out the flames while all the onlookers screamed and shouted with a mixture of excitement and fear. Fortunately, he managed to extinguish the flames before he came to any harm. I was immediately taken down to the headmaster's office where I had to explain myself. There was no real explanation to be given, and I couldn't think of anything to say. Even I knew that there was no excuse for setting fire to a classmate's hair. The headmaster decided that a caning was the appropriate punishment. I refused to submit to him, tore the cane out of his hand and snapped it in half.

"Fuck off, you," I told the headmaster. "I'm not letting you anywhere near me."

"Give me the lighter," he insisted, holding out his hand. "It's confiscated, and don't think that you can come to me to get it back."

"No, I fucking won't."

I loved the lighter because it was one of the few things my father had ever given me, and I considered it a token of his affection. As I walked out of the headmaster's office, he called after me, "Walker, you're expelled until further notice!"

When I told Grandad I wasn't allowed to go back to school until further notice, he went completely mad and started chasing me around the house brandishing a carving knife and shouting, "I'll kill you, you little bastard! I'll bloody well teach you to get into trouble. You want trouble? I'll *give* you trouble!" I ran as fast as I could to escape him but eventually he caught up with me in the lounge. He was red-faced, breathing hard, and appeared to be completely out of control. I became so frightened that I actually lashed out at Grandad, in fear of my own life, and hit him, just the once. I knocked him over. As he tumbled through a jumble of chairs and onto the ground with his mangled arm flapping uselessly, I ran out of the house, afraid of what he might do if he caught up with me.

It wasn't until much later that I decided to go home. I was very frightened, but I had nowhere else to go, and no one would have looked after me. When I got home I was sent up to my room and found myself in dire straits with my uncles and aunts, who had gathered in the house for a family conference because of what had happened. I felt abandoned by them because they sided with Grandad, and because some of them did not believe that Grandad would ever use a knife in such a threatening way. They said that I was lying, or at least exaggerating. Aunties who had always been so kind began to look at me askance. Of course, we all knew that Grandad had a temper, but nobody except me had ever seen him do anything more than scream and shout. This was the first time that he had ever reached for a weapon.

After that, Grandad became more and more abusive and angry with me. Nan, who knew about my reputation at school, was concerned that maybe there was something wrong with me that they had not managed to identify, that maybe I was a head case of some sort and in need of medical help.

"Steve," Nan said. "I'm going to take you to the doctor because if we go on like this it's going to be the death of me." She explained that she thought that maybe there was something wrong with my brain and that she hoped the doctor would be able to fix it.

Nan, like so many people of her generation, had huge respect for all doctors.

Nan took me to the doctor and told him that she was at her wits' end, that I was out of control and that she was very worried about what would become of me. She asked him if there was anything he could do for me; anything at all. The doctor, whom I knew from various childhood ailments, looked at me from across his big mahogany desk. I looked back at him.

"Can you give some examples of his behaviour?" he asked Nan.

"It's just that he's so difficult to control. We can't handle him at all, and he's always in trouble at school. I think there's got to be something wrong with him; it's not normal, that's all."

The doctor asked her a few more questions and then wrote out a prescription for Valium, which he said should calm me down and help me to keep my temper under control. Nan was so upset and worried by that stage that I imagine she would have agreed to a lobotomy if someone had suggested it. Fortunately, they didn't – although lobotomies were still being carried out in those days. I don't remember the doctor asking *me* anything about why I was feeling the way I did.

I was fourteen years old at the time, going on fifteen, and hopeful that the Valium would help, because the prospect of going into the adult world without anything to support me was a horrifying one.

I took the Valium for the next year or so with no noticeable difference. But when I reached the age of sixteen and starting drinking, I found out that mixing Valium and alcohol could get quite a nice little buzz going, a buzz that took the edge off any anxiety or insecurity that I was experiencing and made me feel confident enough to swagger about with the best of them. Valium and alcohol conspired to create a pleasant, drifty feeling that was like falling into a lovely dream in which nothing mattered very much. Together, they worked much better than separately. I was quite impressed and certainly had no resistance to further prescriptions for Valium from then on. The doctor was kind enough to supply them at regular intervals.

I began to wonder what else I could do, what other things I could take, to create similar feelings and sensations to that offered by the combination of Valium and alcohol. I knew that there were various options available on the street, but I had never really looked into it before. Now, I was definitely intrigued.

I was used to my lack of academic achievements, so I made little effort to learn any more. I was a terrible student, rebellious and difficult to deal with. The lessons were far beyond my capabilities, as I was only just capable of writing my name and picking out a few simple words with great effort. Now that I had found another way to relax, I moved away from my sporting endeavours. We all knew that I was just putting in time until I was old enough to leave school, while the teachers came down hard on me in an effort to keep the classroom calm enough for the others to learn. I could not and would not conform to the expectations of the teachers and was quite obnoxious in all my interactions with them.

Underneath all this rebellion, I was very scared – although I would never have admitted it, not to anyone. I was desperately embarrassed and anxious about the fact that I had nothing whatsoever to show for all my years in school. While I liked to swagger and show off around the other kids, I was always afraid that they would bring up the subject of my academic shortcomings and make fun of me. The adult world was fast approaching and I knew that I was in no way prepared for it. I couldn't read or write properly, and I knew that nobody would take me on for an apprenticeship because I was not going to pass any exams.

I was very interested in mechanics – I loved cars and motorbikes – and had a dream of working in that area, but unless something changed radically, that was just not going to happen. Who would want a mechanic who couldn't read? My interest in mechanics had been sparked by Uncle Albie years before, and he continued to foster it now. At this stage, Uncle Albie had a small garage at the back of the Lambeth Mews, just off the Lambeth Walk. He worked there most evenings and weekends on cars or motorbikes, to bring in some extra money. At weekends I was allowed to go and help him.

When I was helping Uncle Albie, I found it a lot easier to stay out of trouble. I had also found something that I was good at. I enjoyed getting my hands dirty and learning about all the different types of engines. I would happily stay there for hours, just watching and learning. It was through Albie that I acquired my first motorbike, an Ariel Colt 200cc, which was rather like a Tiger Cub. It was my pride and joy, and I felt unadulterated happiness when I sat on it.

When I left school, I picked up some work with the firm that had employed me during the summer holidays, Woodcock Brothers in Wimbledon, as well as helping Uncle Albie out whenever I could. It was wonderful to know that my school days were over and that I would not have to put up with the daily torment of sitting uncomprehendingly in a classroom ever again.

Although I was learning some useful skills with my uncle, around this time I started to get involved in petty crime to pay for the booze and the other bits and pieces that I needed, because, as a teenager, I had no way of making as much money as I wanted. Together with some of my mates, I started doing "smash-and-grabs" on local jewellery shops to raise a little cash. This involved breaking the shop window, grabbing a handful of jewellery and legging it down the road before the shop owner had time to realise what was going on.

We knew people on the street who would buy the jewellery, or whatever we had managed to grab, for a fraction of what it was worth, so that they could sell it on and make a decent profit. Sometimes they sold the pieces as they were and sometimes they melted down the gold and silver and sold them as materials. These people were known as "fences". After a successful raid, we'd ring a fence and tell him that we had some goods for him. Because we wanted to get our hands on the money as quickly as possible, they invariably got a great bargain.

I loved doing the smash-and-grabs. The money was secondary, so far as I was concerned. Stealing the stuff and legging it down the road was a fantastic thrill, not unlike the thrill I'd enjoyed as a little kid, playing Knock Down Ginger. Afterwards, when things had calmed down, I would think about what I had done and rationalise it. I told myself that as the shops were insured, I was really stealing from an insurance company, because the shop would be fine; I wasn't stealing from ordinary, decent people, but from big faceless corporations that could deal with the occasional loss. The quantity of money that we managed to make wasn't very impressive, but it was enough to keep us in cheap drinks for a while, and until that old itch and longing for excitement became too big to ignore.

CHAPTER 3

Sex and Drugs and Rock 'n' Roll

My first sexual encounter with a girl was set up by my friends. Because I was still a virgin, they used to take the mickey out of me, always testing my sexual knowledge by asking me questions which of course I couldn't answer. I was very embarrassed about being the butt of their jokes but unsure as to how to rectify the situation as I hadn't met a girl I liked enough to get up the courage to ask her out, and didn't feel confident around women; I found their presence intimidating and confusing.

One evening, we were all on our motorbikes at Attbridge Park when my mates pointed at a nearby wooded area and said, "You need to go over there, Steve. There's a girl called Sheila over there and she wants to talk to you."

I walked over to the woods and met a woman of about twenty-five who told me she wanted to have sex with me. I quickly realised that my mates had paid her to give me a fuck and relieve me of my socially unacceptable virginity. Sheila did the business with me quickly and efficiently. Although I participated, I found the experience totally frightening; I didn't know what to do, and it didn't help that I could hear my mates sniggering in the bushes from where they were watching me.

Once it was all over, Sheila got up, wiped herself off and walked away without a word. It was not a happy time. Putting my clothes back together, I went over to my mates. They were all laughing and kept asking me questions. I was embarrassed and humiliated but did a reasonably good job of covering this up with bravado.

* * *

Fortunately, at this stage, I'd managed to get a new job, and I got stuck in. To be fair to myself, I was not and had never been afraid of hard work. My job was pointing up brickwork for a man called Tony who specialised in building restoration. Tony was in his thirties at the time. He was a big chap who was quite a trendy dresser, and I had a lot of admiration for him. He came from a local family who all worked in the more skilled end of the building trade, and there always seemed to be plenty of work for them. As I had already acquired a lot of labouring experience with the Woodcock Brothers, I picked up pointing skills very quickly, and Tony could see that I was a fast and willing worker.

Despite the fact that I was constantly getting into trouble and had a major problem with authority, Tony liked me. And there was always work for me when I wanted it, regardless of what I had been up to. I am pretty sure that Tony had no idea of how important he was to me; so far as I was concerned, he was much more of a father figure to me than my actual father had ever been. He tried very hard with me and did his best to keep me in a safe place. He kept in touch with my grandparents, and between them they tried to concert their efforts to keep me on the straight and narrow.

For a while, working for Tony gave me the hope that I might be able to build a normal life, despite all my deficits. I was pleased to discover that I was well able to learn the skills that Tony needed me to have and that I turned out to be quite good at the tasks he assigned to me. It meant a lot when Tony praised something that I had done, and on those days I would go home with a great feeling of satisfaction. But despite this flicker of hope, I still wanted and felt that I needed the excitement and thrill of everything to do with the wrong side of the tracks.

I was increasingly curious about the wide array of illegal drugs available on the street. Considering how much I had enjoyed my experiments with mixing Valium and booze, I was eager to learn more and pleased when my forays into illegal drug-taking proved to be as pleasant and exciting as I had hoped they would. One problem, though, was that I needed more money than I was making from the jobs I did for Tony. He paid me a fair wage, but the drugs I wanted were expensive, and my appetite for them voracious.

From grabbing the occasional bit of jewellery, I graduated to stealing motorbikes, which was more exciting and offered a great deal more in terms of thrills. I was still very interested in mechanics and vehicles in general. I had become friendly with a bunch of lads who were slightly older than me. They were making what seemed to me to be a pretty decent living robbing people and stealing from shops, and I was very attracted to them and their way of life. To me it seemed almost magical, and doing that sort of thing clearly gave them a buzz that lasted longer than the one I got from mixing Valium and alcohol.

I was taking a lot of drugs at this time, often together with my new friends, and I could see no reason not to join them, although Brian, always a good and loyal friend, told me that I was being stupid and that I would end up getting into serious trouble if I wasn't careful. Much as I liked and respected him in general, I didn't care what Brian thought. For one thing, stealing was a way to make a meaningful amount of money. While Tony offered me a route to full-time work and a decent salary, I certainly wasn't going to get rich by pointing up brickwork.

I found out that, just like with drugs, the more you get involved with stealing and general law-breaking, the more you want to continue with it because it's exciting, it's fun and there is a real high involved in knowing that you've got away with it. And, as stupid as it might seem, I felt that getting away with it meant in some way that I was getting a dig at anyone who had ever done me any wrong, and that I was evening up the cosmic score. It wasn't *my* fault that I had been born into a messed-up family, was it? People luckier than me had done nothing to deserve their good fortune. What made someone else deserve a nice house and an expensive motorbike when I had to live in my grandparents' tiny house? It wasn't fair; if fate had been kinder to me, I would have those things, too – maybe more. By taking things that didn't belong to me, by taking things that belonged to people who were luckier and more blessed than I was, I was just making the world that little bit fairer. That was the way I saw it.

I was still working for Tony Spooner, and he watched with dismay as I spiralled out of control, despite all his best efforts on my behalf and despite his insistence that I was a good lad, really, notwithstanding all the evidence to the contrary. Tony kept telling me, "Son, you're in the wrong area. You shouldn't be doing this; you shouldn't be hanging out with those guys, they'll end up causing you nothing but trouble. You're a good lad at heart and I know it. Stick with me and I will show you how to earn your living honestly. Forget about them; they are a bad influence on you."

I would say, "Yeah, yeah, right…" but we both knew that I was paying him no attention whatsoever.

I never understood what I did to make Tony care so much. But he was genuinely fond of me, and had been ever since he took me on to work for him shortly after I left school. Although I wanted very much to impress Tony and make him proud, I also loved the feelings I got from taking drugs, anything from prescription drugs to what was available illegally on the street: amphetamines, nembies or sleepers, LSD, dope, mandies, dexies, purple hearts and anything else I could get my hands on.

I learned how to use the drugs together. If you've been on a lot of speed, for example, you can take sleepers to slow the comedown and make it easier to deal with. If you are drinking, you can take mandies – Mandrax is its brand name when sold legally – with the booze for an interesting buzz. For each drug that was available, there was a different type of high. There was always the risk that it wouldn't go quite as you had planned. With LSD, for instance, you never knew if the hallucinations it would give you were going to be good or bad. That risk was part of the thrill.

Everything was taken out of my control and I just gave myself up to the substances and the experiences they gave me. Mostly, these experiences were wonderful. The drugs I took brought me a feeling of release and calm that was unlike anything else and far better than the approval of my elders or the satisfaction of a pay cheque at the end of the week. They made me feel like the man I wanted to be, and not the pathetic kid I actually was.

Aged about seventeen, I started going out with a girl called Kate, who lived in Wallington in Surrey. Kate was very pretty and sweet, and she was something of a childhood sweetheart. I can still remember her smile. We had met at the Green in Carshalton, which was where the rockers used to hang out in their cool clothes, trying to impress passers-by with how tough they were. I had long hair and I wore a leather jacket with studs, greasy jeans and hobnail boots. I felt I fitted in with the crowd and that I looked cool. I had a number of tattoos done and was very pleased with the result; I felt that they were a considerable enhancement to my look. I was quite good-looking, so the girls paid attention to me, which was nice.

Most of the guys knocking around the Green were hard men looking for a fight, especially with the crew from Mitcham, who were our enemies. We quite regularly got involved in gang fights and would set up meets to have a pre-arranged battle. Everyone would get stuck in using lumps of wood, motorcycle chains, boots and anything else they could find. Some people got really hurt, but that's just the way it was. We were boys on a mission and we weren't going to let anyone get in our way.

I was friendly with the guys for a while, but drifted away when I saw how the men treated the women in their group, which was just awful. Despite, or maybe even because of the fact that I had never known my mother, I was quite protective of women, even as a teenager, and I was genuinely horrified when I found out that these guys were treating the girls like sex objects, passing them around among themselves and making fun of them afterwards.

I think it was the girls' vulnerability that really got to me. I could relate to it, having been vulnerable myself from a young age, and I didn't like to watch it happening, or to hear the girls being laughed at. Kate was one of the girls they misused, and when we started going out we both broke away from that group and stayed away from that lifestyle.

Kate was a tall, confident girl with lovely blonde hair and a bright, intelligent face. She had been adopted by a fairly well-to-do family, with a big house and a comfortable standard of living. They had given her a good home and childhood, but Kate had a lot of unresolved issues about being an adopted child. In those days, adoption wasn't discussed as openly as it is now, and any negative feelings about it would have been very much swept under the carpet. Now that she was a teenager, Kate was going through a rebellious phase and making a point by hanging around the park with unsavoury rockers.

I was very happy with Kate, and for a while it seemed as though this lovely relationship was all I needed to help me to go straight, because she made me feel wanted, and she made me feel good. I still had a big problem with my temper, and there were still times when I would boil up over something very small and lose control, but Kate was a steadying influence on me. She helped me to calm down, and I was able to take fewer drugs than before. Things were wonderful.

Once in a while, Kate would become convinced that I had got her pregnant, but then her period would come and we would be relieved to know that it had just been a false alarm. With each pregnancy scare that came and went, I became less worried that anything untoward would actually happen. So far as I was concerned, the future looked very rosy.

Initially, Kate's parents were kind and welcoming to me. It wasn't until I started getting caught doing the smash-and-grabs that they started telling her that I was an idiot and that she would be better off without me. I didn't care. Kate was mine and I was hers. What did her parents' opinion matter?

It all went horribly wrong when some of the Carshalton guys started hanging around with Kate again, and she became involved with one of them behind my back. The boy in question was a mate of mine, Eric. Eric had nowhere to live at the time, and Nan had said that he could stay with us for a while. This made Kate's betrayal a thousand times worse. She hadn't just been screwing around behind my back; she'd been doing it with a mate whom I had trusted and let into my home. That was the end of two relationships: the one with Kate and the one with Eric.

The one good thing that happened was that although Eric was a hard man, I found out that I was much harder than him. I had always been a little scared of Eric, but now that he had pissed me off, I tore into him and beat him to a bloody pulp, finding energy and drive I didn't even know I had. It felt great, standing over him with my sore fists and looking at him where he lay crumpled on the floor. He got what he deserved.

Kate and Eric didn't stay together, so in the end neither of us got her. I was still absolutely devastated by what I saw as Kate's betrayal and just went berserk in reaction to it. I smashed things up and I had a run-in with Kate when I told her exactly what I thought of her. I thought she was the lowest of the low. She had deceived me. I had believed that she and I had something special and now I felt as though all my efforts and hard work in keeping the relationship going were being thrown back in my face. I took whatever drugs I could get my hands on to take my mind off the fact that Kate had cheated on me and in the hope that they would fix my broken heart.

At this time, I used to hang about in a café in Rose Hill; a greasy spoon that was enjoying unaccountable popularity in the area. It was a place where the kids used to hang out during the day and the evening, to play pinball and the juke box. It was mainly frequented by youngsters and barrow boys, the usual rough-and-ready crowd, most of them involved in petty crime of one kind or another. On one particular evening, shortly after the bust-up with Kate, I was in there and at a very low ebb, when I met my friend Lenny, who offered me some speed. Lenny wasn't really a dealer, just one of the many slightly shady characters I knew from the street. He wasn't pushing drugs on me, just trying to help me out.

"Come on, mate," Lenny said, having given me a pep talk about Kate and everything that had happened between us. "They will make you feel better in a jiffy. It's just what you need right now. Trust me. What have you got to lose, anyway?"

I decided that I had nothing to lose and I took him up on his offer. I quickly discovered that Lennie was absolutely right because, thanks to speed, I soon felt fantastic. All my worries and concerns and fears went away. I felt very good about myself and had no insecurities at all, despite the fact that I actually had a hell of a lot to feel insecure about.

On speed, I was confident and chatty and came out of my shell. Everybody liked me better when I was using speed. I liked myself better, too. Obviously, I thought, speed was what I had needed all this time. If I had known about speed earlier, things would have worked out better for me. I would have been able to focus, and I wouldn't have let Kate humiliate me. To hell with Valium and booze.

I started to take speed more regularly and at least for a while I was happier and more confident than I had ever been before. My behaviour was more stable than ever and, although I wasn't sleeping, but staying up all night partying and being crazy, I felt that I had found the medication I needed. Clearly, I was better informed than any doctor. While the Valium had numbed my senses and made me feel stupid, speed made me feel alert, clued in and clever. Speed was very cheap in those days; I think you could get twenty tablets for a pound. It was an easy habit to maintain, even for a kid on a modest and erratic income, and I was able to keep myself in speed without that many smash-and-grabs.

Because I was so happy and confident now, I became a bit of a leader among the group of guys that I used to hang about with, and one by one they began to follow my example and experiment with speed. They had already grown used to sharing my Valium when we went out, and when they saw how good I felt on speed, following suit was the next logical step. One or two were wise enough to experiment a little and then decide that enough was enough, but some of the others had as much fun as I did and proceeded to experiment with other drugs, too.

Chapter 4

Leaving Home

When my grandparents realised how deeply involved with drug-taking I had become, they kicked me out and told me that I was on my own now. If I was going to break the law and screw things up, I could do it without running back to them every time I needed a hot meal and a shoulder to cry on. Although Grandad was usually the one who liked to lay down the law, Nan was the one who told me that I had to leave home. She was upset and red-eyed the day she called me into the kitchen for a chat.

"Stevie," she said. "You've got to go. We just can't live with you any more. You've got to sort yourself out."

Nan and Grandad were getting old. They knew they couldn't deal with me any longer. They were sick of seeing me coming home after a bender and crashing out for three days. They were sick of wondering when they would see me again, and whether I'd be all bruised up or not. They didn't know how they could help me, and had reached the stage at which they knew they just had to do what was best for them.

"That's fine," I said. "I don't care."

"And Steve," Nan said. "Try to stay away from those friends of yours. They're no good and you'll just end up getting into even more trouble."

My grandparents understandably felt that they should no longer have to be responsible for someone who kept getting himself into scrapes. Nan liked to think that "bad company" was responsible for all of my bad decisions. She had often said, "Steve, you're a good boy really, I know you are. But you're easily led. You just need to learn how to stay away from bad company."

As well as just needing some time and space away from me and the chaos I inevitably brought home, I imagine that Nan and Grandad may have felt that a short, sharp shock was what I needed to help me get myself under control, and that being asked to leave home might be just the ticket.

At first, I had no idea where to go. Then I remembered my best friend, Brian, who had a car. Although Brian didn't approve of my drug-taking or general bad behaviour, he was a great friend and he was always there for me. I went round to his place and asked him if I could use his car to kip in for a little while, and he said that that was OK. For a number of weeks I lived outside Brian's house in his white Sunbeam Rapier Convertible. It was winter and I remember trying to sleep in the back, wrapped up in a blanket, but being unable to do so because I was so cold. It didn't help that the back window was made of torn PVC.

Brian's mum knew that I was sleeping outside in the car, but did nothing either to stop me or to invite me in. By now, I had figured out that she had a drinking or a psychiatric problem. She was a recluse who almost never left the house. I was one of the few people Brian knew who was trusted enough to step through their front door. He was usually very wary of people meeting his mum and seeing what his domestic situation was like. I was perfectly happy to sleep in the car, not wanting to impose myself on anybody, or ask questions that they might not want to answer.

I was not completely cut off from my grandparents at this stage, and I still went home once in a while for a meal and a wash. They fed me and put up with me occasionally, but they weren't that keen on seeing me, which was fair enough; they had done all they could for me and I had repaid them by throwing it back in their faces. I wasn't even pretending not to be taking drugs any more. This was my way of life now, and I didn't really care who knew about it.

Even though Nan steadfastly maintained that all my problems were the fault of the nameless people who she considered were leading me astray, they must both have been very disappointed with how I had turned out. At the time, I gave little or no thought to how they were feeling because I was busy with my

young life; with impressing my friends and acquaintances, growing my hair, listening to music – I still
loved music and it was one of the few things that gave
me some time out from all the hassle – taking drugs
and doing whatever it took to get my hands on the
funds to continue doing so.

* * *

After a while, I moved into my own flat in Wallington,
about six or seven miles from Carshalton. I'd managed
to get a little money together myself, but I'd borrowed
the money for the deposit from Tony. I was on probation at the time for stealing a motorbike. I hadn't
really stolen a bike, but had been driving one of Brian's
around without a licence or insurance. It was actually
a bike that the two of us had been building together.
Well, as I was still a minor, when I got caught I knew
that if I told the truth Brian would get the rap for it,
so I said that I had stolen the bike, and I was nicked.
I was arrested for TDA – Take and Drive Away – and
put on probation for twelve months.

I loved the flat. It was at the top of a tall building
and had its own little kitchen, its own little living
room and a bedroom. It was just for me, and I was
determined to keep it nice. Grandad had trained
me well, and I was always very neat and orderly. I
smoked a lot, both joints and cigarettes, and I went
to immense effort to ensure that there was always
an ashtray in place. I emptied the ashtrays regularly,

because it mattered a lot to me that everything was clean and proper. My friends would come over and I would fuss around them, making them take their shoes off, not letting them throw their things around and endlessly removing ashtrays to empty them.

"Cor, Steve," they would say, "you've got your own place; what do you want to be fussing over everything for?" I would just keep tidying up around them, because the one thing I hated more than anything was a mess. It was a relief to me when my mates moved on or when we decided to go out to a concert, because I couldn't stand it when the flat became untidy. We went to lots of concerts. I saw The Rolling Stones at Hyde Park when they were in their strutting glory days, and I used to go to the Coliseum and a lot of the clubs on Wardour Street, such as the Temple. At the flat, I had graduated from a record player to a cassette player and listened to my favourite bands all the time.

I repaid Tony's generosity with the deposit, and with countless other things, by working hard and well when I was actually at work, but I ignored the rest of his good advice and even began to resent it a little. Who was he, to tell me what to do? What did he think he was? He wasn't my father. He wasn't anything to me. He had no business trying to tell me how to run my life. I was a grown-up now and I could make my own decisions, with no help from anyone. I paid Tony little attention.

I saw my father occasionally during this period, albeit mostly when I was in serious trouble and had nowhere else to turn. By now he had settled down somewhat and was living with a woman called Theresa, who was doing her level best to keep him calm. Theresa was a good woman and, although I never got to know her very well, I had a lot of respect for her because I knew how difficult Dad was, and what she must have had to put up with from him.

More than my father, Theresa did what she could to help me out when I got into trouble yet again. She did this out of the goodness of her heart. When I went round to their house, it was usually on a Saturday, and Dad would be down at the pub having a few jars. After the pub he would go to the bookies' to place a few bets, and after that he would come home and want to watch the racing on the telly, to see whether or not he had won any money. Despite the fact that he always lost much more than he won, he never lost his interest in gambling. Dad had no interest in conversation, least of all with me. My father was prepared to tolerate me, but not interested enough to exchange more than a few words.

In those days, very few people owned their televisions; they used to rent them, instead. Televisions were expensive then, and more likely to break than they are now. It was a lot easier to rent. Dad rented his from an outfit called Radio Rentals, which had a little shop just down the road from his house. One day, his telly wasn't working when there was an important race on that he wanted to watch. He went down to Radio Rentals and said, "My fucking television isn't working and I want to watch the horse racing. I'll give you half an hour to get down to my house and fix it and if you don't, I'll throw it out the fucking window."

Half an hour passed and no repair man came. So Dad threw the telly unceremoniously out the window. It hit the road hard and broke into pieces. I thought that this was hilarious and we both cracked up laughing in a rare display of father-and-son solidarity. When the repair man finally came round to fix the broken television, Dad went to the door and said, "So you're here at last, are you? Well, the fucking telly's in the road, so fix it. And if you can't fix it, give me another one."

I remember feeling great admiration for my dad that day, for standing up for himself and not letting anyone muck him around. This was the sort of thing that I felt I should do too whenever anyone got in my way.

I don't know if my father and Theresa were happy together, but she was a strong person and the only one who was ever able to even come close to managing him. I imagine that Dad was as happy then as he ever was. Theresa still had her work cut out, though. Dad was a very jealous, possessive man and if he thought anyone was looking at her when they went out together, he was all over them like a rash before they had a chance to deny it. Dad would always pick a fight if he thought that people were looking at his woman.

When Theresa was out at work, where Dad couldn't control who looked at her, he got very anxious because anything could be going on, and there was nothing he could do about it. He always had to know what time she expected to be home, and if she was late, he had to know why she was late so that he could be sure that she wasn't really out with another man, getting up to no good behind his back. He was clearly desperately insecure, because Theresa had given him every reason to trust and respect her.

Over the years, Dad lost a lot of friends because of his violent, possessive nature. The moment he thought that someone had trespassed on his area, he was furious, even if it was someone he had been friends with for years. He didn't care; he just lashed out with all he had and worried about the consequences later, if at all.

Very occasionally, however, Dad did something nice. When I bought a silver Honda CB72, he blew me away by agreeing to be named as the guarantor on the hire-purchase agreement. This was an incredible bike. It had been built by Frank Dunstall, a name you will know if you are interested in road racing. My new bike had rear sets, goldies, clip-ons, American cams and American springs that allowed the engine to run around 1,200 revs per minute, rather than 9,500. When I rode that amazing bike, I felt and looked like a film star; I really did. Even with a part exchange on my previous bike, a red and chrome Royal Enfield Crusader Sports, I would never have been able to get it without Dad's help. To this day I am surprised that he agreed to my request.

CHAPTER 5

Love and Marriage?

After things ended with Kate, my first love, I had gone through a very bad patch, so far as girls and women were concerned. I had been very attracted to Kate, because she was so pretty, but what I mostly wanted was for her to devote herself to me, to sacrifice her own interests and to be there for me unquestioningly, regardless of what I did, and what happened. I had been desperate for love and affection but, like my father, if I didn't get what I wanted, I was liable to become aggressive and even violent, although most of my self-destructiveness was aimed firmly at myself.

Jane was a leggy, beautiful blonde, a year or two older than me, who lived in my area. I used to ride past her house on my motorbike on my way home. By now, I was riding my Honda CB72, which had very distinctive-sounding exhaust pipes that attracted attention on the street. I might have felt like shit about being dumped by Kate, but at least I had my bike.

I had seen Jane emerging from her house on a few occasions and one day I decided to stop my bike and talk to her. My first thought on seeing her was, "I want her; she is a tasty bird." She was the sort of woman who turned heads when she walked down the street; the kind of girl who made other men jealous when they saw her and knew she was with somebody else. She had a great figure, bright blonde hair that bounced on her shoulders and a very pretty face. My idea was that if I could get a woman of that calibre to go out with me, it would mean that I was someone worth looking up to. To be honest, I also thought it would put Kate's nose out of joint when she found out that I had a new girl, as I was still smarting about the end of our relationship.

I managed to persuade Jane to go out with me, and I took her to the St Helier Arms, one of the roughest pubs in the area, on our first date. The St Helier Arms was on the same street as Jane's house, Greenwave Lane, so she knew all about it. I was proud of the fact that I was accepted in St Helier's, among some of the toughest criminals in the neighbourhood, even though I was small fry at this stage. It wasn't long before Jane and I started seeing each other regularly. I could see her whenever I wanted, because she wasn't working at the time and was always available.

I met her family and seemed to get on quite well with them. Jane was from an ordinary working-class family with two brothers and a sister. Her mum was a nurse but her dad wasn't able to work. So far as I could figure out from what Jane said, he had a mental health issue of some sort and was plagued by regular breakdowns. One of Jane's brothers was still at school, and the other, Gary, worked as a hairdresser and cultivated friendships with some of the shadier members of the neighbourhood. Like me, he was a regular at the St Helier Arms.

I've often thought about how hearing music can bring any memory back to mind. Today, when I hear the tracks that I listened to at this phase in my life, and later on, I am immediately returned to the past. Just by listening to specific songs, I can recall very clearly where I was, who I was with, what I was wearing and particularly what drugs I was using at the time. Today, when I listen to tracks by The Rolling Stones or The Beatles, I know that I would have been using LSD and amphetamines back then, because I felt that these drugs complemented the music very well. When I listened to Hendrix, I used coke, speed and dope.

I went to loads of gigs at this stage of my life. I particularly remember going to see Golden Earring at Fairfield Halls in Croydon. I dropped two tabs of white lightning, or LSD, while my mates and I listened to the band, danced with everyone else, and generally had a wonderful time. I remember clearly popping the tablets into my mouth and the sensation of them immediately dissolving. Within minutes, I felt completely on top of the world and really into what was going on around me. Thanks to the acid, all my senses were heightened. The band was accompanied by a light show, and the drugs made it absolutely magnificent, while the combination of the music and the acid made me tremble all over.

By the time the show ended and everyone started filing out to go home, I was unbelievably spaced out. The plan had been that we would all go back to my flat and spend the rest of the evening smoking dope and listening to music. However, on the way back I somehow became separated from my friends and ended up at home on my own, completely out of my head. I still remember very clearly letting myself into the flat and finding everything so quiet that it was spooky and frightening.

I calmed myself, sat down and put on some music. Jane had a pet dog, a boxer, Rover, who was spending the night in the flat and was probably quite lonely. He came over to me to be petted. He reached up and licked my face. As he did so, his face seemed to grow and spread until it looked as though Rover was big enough to swallow me whole.

"Christ," I thought, "Rover's fucking tongue is bigger than my whole head." I was completely freaked out.

"Enough is enough," I decided. "I'll take some downers to get back to normal." I took a couple of Tuinal out of my pocket and swallowed them. After a while these started to work, by slowing my metabolism down, and I went to sleep.

Meanwhile, my old girlfriend Kate called over to Nan's house to tell her that she was pregnant and that

I was the father. She had told me that she was pregnant so many times in the course of our relationship that I assumed this was just one more false alarm that would come to nothing, so I ignored it.

Well, that was my mistake. It turned out that it hadn't been another false alarm, after all. Kate duly gave birth to a little boy, my first child. We named the child Lee, but he took Kate's surname. Kate and I fell out and I didn't see Lee very often. I didn't know how much I wanted to be involved in his life and I had no idea where I was going or what I was doing. I accepted that I was the baby's father, but did not think at any length about what that meant in terms of my responsibilities towards him. I met Kate and Lee in the park a few times and played with him, but I was a terrible father and not really that interested in my son. After a while, even this contact petered out, which meant that I was doing just what my parents had done: having a child and then not taking care of it.

I was still angry with Kate about the way she had behaved towards me and for having betrayed me, and I didn't really want to have anything to do with her or the baby, which I considered to be her affair, not mine. I abandoned my first child without so much as giving it a second thought. I was summoned to court and told that I would have to pay child support. I had no intention of doing anything of the sort. I remember the day I went to court vividly; I was full of indignation and self-righteousness. Who did Kate think she was, trying to get money out of me?

"Well, Mr Walker," the judge said. "You seem to be doing quite well for yourself. You have a good job and you have a nice flat. I can't understand why you're not paying your maintenance money."

I was cheeky. "I'm not paying for something on the hire purchase that I never get to see," I said.

Kate and I weren't getting on by this stage and I never saw the baby.

"Well," said the judge, "your lovely little flat will probably soon have bars around it."

I didn't stay at the flat much longer, because I didn't want to end up behind bars. As soon as my relationship with Jane became established I moved into her place to get away from the maintenance and the whole situation. I never saw Lee again.

I was reasonably happy living at Jane's. I got along quite well with her mum and her brothers, Gary the hairdresser and Joe. Jane's mum was kind and understanding, although I never knew exactly how she felt about our relationship. She seemed to realise that it didn't matter what she said to us or how she told her daughter to behave, because we would just do our own thing anyway.

A nurse, Jane's mother knew that I was involved in taking drugs, and of course she wanted me to stop, because she was aware of the dangers involved. She tried to be supportive in helping me sort out my addiction, but while I gave the impression of going along with it, I didn't see the drugs as a problem.

A few months passed, and I decided that Jane and I should get married as soon as possible. I was still seventeen at the time, coming up to eighteen. I obtained an engagement ring from the Freeman's catalogue that my auntie Pat ran. The Freeman's catalogue sold all sorts of things through a hire-purchase scheme. I never paid Auntie Pat the money I owed her for the ring.

"Do you want to get married?" I asked Jane. I proudly showed her the ring that I had bought. She said yes, so I gave her the ring and decided to proceed with the marriage as soon as possible. Jane went along with it, although she never seemed entirely convinced of the whole idea. I believe one of the reasons Jane was keen to marry was that she wanted to leave home and get away from her parents, especially her dad, whose psychiatric problems made him difficult to live with.

We set a date for the wedding, and Jane and I got married at a church in Rose Hill. I smartened myself up and wore a jacket and trousers. Jane was traditional, in white. My best man Brian, who had never been involved with drugs and was increasingly concerned about me and disapproving of my behaviour, failed to turn up. He had told me when we got engaged that he didn't believe that Jane and I loved each other and that we were getting married for all the wrong reasons. "I'm not going to be a part of that farce," he said. I hadn't quite believed him until he didn't show on the day. Fortunately, I was carrying the wedding ring myself, so I got somebody else to stand in at the last minute.

It was strange, seeing my side of the church so empty. Even Nan and Grandad hadn't come. Auntie Pat was the only person from my family to come, although she had questioned my decision and said that she didn't think the marriage was a good idea. At the time, though, I honestly didn't care what anyone thought about me or anything I did. My feeling was that it didn't matter. Life was what it was and you just had to deal with it one day at a time. I mostly dealt with it by taking amphetamines.

Of Jane's family, only her brother Gary turned up, and he walked her down the aisle. It was not a good start to married life. We all went down the pub afterwards for a drink, and that was that.

After our marriage, Jane and I went back to live in her parents' house for a while. This was supposed to be a temporary measure, until we organised our own place. I didn't mind living with her parents for a little while and they were extremely patient with me, considering that I was the teenage drug addict who had just married their daughter against everyone's good judgement. Jane's mum was supportive of me, although she must have been concerned about what my heavy drug-taking and erratic behaviour meant for her daughter.

When I broke down with speed psychosis as a result of my amphetamine abuse, she took me to St George's Hospital in Tooting, where I was registered as an addict. Speed psychosis is like temporary schizophrenia. My imagination ran wild and I could hear voices telling me things, even though nobody was talking to me. When I calmed down, I was put on Dextroamphetamine Spansules, which were time-release capsules of amphetamines that were supposed to keep me under control by releasing the drug gradually into my bloodstream.

Fortunately, I had learned something from my experience with Kate, and Jane and I were sensible about birth control, so at least she didn't get knocked up. I was hardly in a position to be a good father.

Two weeks after the wedding, I was arrested for robbery and put on remand in Ashford in Kent. I was very definitely guilty as charged. I had been trying to get some extra money together so that Jane and I could get a flat of our own, and stealing was the brightest idea that I had come up with. I think I thought Jane would respect me more if I was able to come up with the cash without help from anyone, and I knew that I wanted to get out of living with her parents as soon as possible. I did a smash-and-grab at a local jewellery shop with a couple of friends. The robbery was poorly planned and badly executed: I crashed the getaway car straight into a police car that was in pursuit.

So instead of moving into my first home as part of a married couple, it was the detention centre for me. Considering how I was apprehended, I could hardly plead innocent, so I pleaded guilty and got six months. My friends claimed innocence, but ended up getting put away for twelve and eighteen months.

I was sent to Latchmere House, which was considered to be the hardest detention centre for young offenders out there. I got there by police bus and entered a completely different world. Arriving in reception, I could not believe my eyes. Or my ears, for that matter. A screw – what we called the prison guards – came up to me and stuck his big, red face in mine.

"From now on," he said, "everything I say, you say, 'Yes, sir, no, sir, three bags full, sir'. Have you got that?"

I was full of bravado. "Since when have you been fucking knighted?" I asked. "If you want to be called 'sir', maybe you should think about *that*."

His face grew even redder as he took in my words and then he bellowed at me, spit flying from the corners of his mouth, leaving me in no doubt whatsoever as to who was boss.

Giving cheek to the screw was my first big mistake. In places like Latchmere House, the screws stick together and I had just guaranteed myself a hard time for the entire duration of my stay.

My cell was quite a dismal place with one bed, one cupboard, one piss pot and one chair. Everything had to be folded up or put away neatly every day. I had to square my blankets off and polish my floor. My cell was spotless, because my grandfather had taught me well and I hated it when things were dirty or disorderly. The point of detention was that I would be given the rehabilitation that I needed, and would have the time and space to focus on my educational deficits.

I was furious and felt very demeaned about being kept locked up and had little or no interest in working towards anything. I was angry, fiery and difficult to deal with, because I found it impossible to contain my resentment and rage. Once again, I found myself in a situation in which I was under threat, and it soon got out of hand. One day, another inmate and I started to fight in the cable shop – where copper was stripped out of lead pipe and cables. We had been working with chisels and club hammers, so there were plenty of weapons to hand. The argument had started over comments that he had been making about Jane.

Jane, my wife, never came to see me, which was bad enough, and now this bastard was saying that she was a slag and that she was sleeping around behind my back. I could not let that lie. I went to smash his head in with a club hammer, to teach him a lesson that he wouldn't forget. I was removed from the cable shop and taken down to the block where we served solitary confinement.

After a few days, I was allowed back to the normal routine, but it had been decided that I should be taken to see some doctors and psychiatrists to see if they could figure out what was wrong with me, and why I consistently acted without thinking. I was sent to a hospital in London to have ECGs and other tests, to try to determine where my unstable behaviour originated, and whether there might be treatments and medications that could help. I didn't mind going; in fact, it was quite nice to have some time away from Latchmere and all its rules and regulations.

I stayed in hospital for three or four days and remember lighting up under the noses of two of the prison guards while the doctors were talking to me.

"Oy!" said one of the guards. "He's not allowed to smoke, you know. They're not allowed to smoke while they're in detention."

"Well," said the doctor. "He's not in detention now. He's in hospital. So he can smoke if he wants to."

So far as the tests went, I just took everything in my stride. For as long as I could remember, people had been suggesting that there was something wrong with me, but I felt that I was reacting normally to the things that happened in my life. I was prepared to be poked and prodded and prescribed medication, but I didn't really know what it was all supposed to be about.

The doctors decided that the left side of my brain was not working as quickly as the right one, creating a sort of psychological imbalance that was leading to my erratic behaviour. I have never found out if there was any truth to this theory or not, but it was very clear that something was definitely wrong. I was prescribed Largactil, to help get my unruly emotions under control. This is considered now to be a "liquid cosh". Most people who take it find that it completely knocks them out, leaving them in a rather zombie-like condition. I can't say it had a strong effect on me, maybe because I was already so very used to mind-altering substances. Despite being on Largactil, back in detention I continued to work out in the gym and to behave pretty much as I always did. I took the drug for the whole time I was serving my sentence.

On entering detention, I had been told that I should use this time to further my education. Sick and tired of putting in time at school to little or no effect, I decided that I would devote myself to physical education. All the inmates had to attend some classes, but they could choose what to focus on, and I decided that body-building and fitness would be my thing. The only obligatory classes were religious instruction, presumably in the hope of instilling some morals into us. It had little impact on me either way. I had no idea what I did or didn't believe in, and the Church of England instructor was not particularly engaging.

I used my time in detention to get physically fit and strong. The atmosphere was very controlled at the detention centre, and for a kid who couldn't read there was very little to do to pass the time and alleviate boredom. I felt hungry for physical exercise and went to the gym every day, often for hour upon hour. I did colour circuits every day. These were training regimes, with the colour identifying how intensive the course was. Black was the hardest and yellow the easiest. I started out with yellow and quickly worked my way up to black. I pressed weights and watched with approval as my body became stronger and more muscular. I had always had a low opinion of myself in general, so it was nice to feel accepting of the way I looked, at least. By the time I had served my sentence and I could go home, I was stronger than I had ever been and extremely fit. I was like a bull. I was ready to take anybody on and confident that I could win. I felt like the cock of the walk.

My grandparents had visited me faithfully throughout my sentence. Perhaps they had told me to leave Jane, and had refused to come to my wedding, but blood is thicker than water, and Nan in particular clung – despite all the evidence to the contrary – to the view that I was a good lad, really. I was in Richmond, which wasn't that far away from Carshalton, but it was a bit of a trek for them because they were getting on in years and beginning to get a little frail.

They must also have been growing tired of hearing that their grandson was in trouble yet again. Every time they came I would get quite upset and promise to be good when I got out. I would feel awfully sorry for myself and desperate to have a life of my own again. I would blame everyone else for the situation that I was in. I didn't think about how difficult I had made things for the elderly couple that had always done the very best they could for me and who now sat in front of me. I took as my divine right the fact that they would come to visit with presents and treats to make my stay behind bars that little bit easier. I expected no less and gave nothing in return.

While I was serving my sentence, I was served with divorce papers. Jane cited the non-consummation of the marriage as grounds for ending it. The fact that I was unable to read the documentation made me even angrier. Even when it was read to me, I struggled to understand the legal language and the full implications of what had happened. At the same time, I knew that there wasn't much I could do about it. By now I had found out that Jane had been sleeping with a bloke called Mickey, whom I already hated. This made it even worse. I felt very low, completely rejected, and it hurt much more than any beating would have. It was even worse than when Kate had left me, because I'd thought that the whole point of my relationship with Jane had been to make me feel better about myself. Now I felt even worse than I had before we got together.

My interest in Jane in the first instance had been spurred by a desire to increase my status. Her leaving me like this made me feel like a worthless piece of shit. I handled the situation very badly and started pumping iron like there was no tomorrow, with the poorly thought-out idea that if I was strong, fit and muscle-bound, I would be in a better position to take care of myself the next time shit happened. I might be a pitiful figure of fun, but at least I didn't have to look like one.

To be fair, the people at the detention centre did try to help me. They knew I was illiterate, and efforts were made to help me address this. But I just didn't give a damn about that any more; I had resigned myself to being thick and had decided that while I couldn't read or write, I could focus on being physically fit and strong and on fighting my way through every difficult situation. I put in the time, managed not to learn anything at all and was finally allowed to go back to where I had come from. I came out of Latchmere and went back to Carshalton to Nan's for a while, picking up some work on the buildings with Tony Spooner.

Now that I was out, my friends were quick to tell me everything that Jane had been getting up to while I was away. Apparently, she had been messing around with some of the guys that I knew – not just Mickey, which had already been bad enough. I had been made a laughing stock! Jane and I had been far too young to get married, and it had just been a game to her, but I was furious and felt that I had been belittled and humiliated and that I had lost face and honour among my peers. Every time I heard someone laughing as I walked down the street, I was sure that I was the object of their ridicule. I became determined to search Jane out and make her pay dearly for what I saw as a personal slight against me.

I already sported some tattoos, but now that I was eighteen, I decided to have a few more. One day, I met my mate Kenny at the Elephant and Castle, and we decided it would be a great idea to have a tattoo each. We found a tattooist, and Kenny went first. He had two small snakes tattooed discreetly behind his ears. Then it was my turn. In my wisdom, and under the influence of alcohol, I decided to have a spider tattooed on each hand. Not one of my better decisions, I have to say, but I have learned to live with them.

Within a few months, I was taking drugs heavily again, mostly amphetamines, and getting myself into a terrible state of rage whenever anything happened that I didn't like. People told me to forget about Jane, that time heals all wounds and that eventually I wouldn't care about her or feel bad any more. They told me that I would meet someone else and that there were plenty more fish in the sea. But I couldn't do it; I couldn't move on. I was obsessed with how bad she had made me feel and how much I wanted to get my revenge on her.

I organised a car, a Morris Isis, and obtained a snub-nose revolver that had started life as a starting pistol and was later honed to fire bullets. I liked the weight of the gun in my hand, and the smooth feel of the metal. It was easy to find out who would sell me a gun, and one of my friends had been only too pleased to help, no questions asked and no explanations required. I thought that I would use the gun to hurt Jane and frighten her. For the moment it just felt good to know that I had a weapon and would be able to look after myself, whatever came up.

A couple of months later, I was driving about in my untaxed, uninsured banger when I saw Jane walking down London Road towards Mitcham. All that blonde loveliness seemed to be taunting me with each step. "You cheating, double-crossing bitch," I thought. "I'll be fucking having you."

I saw red as the mist descended. I mounted the kerb in my car and tried to run her down. I wasn't thinking consciously about killing her; I just wanted to make sure that she couldn't walk down the street with her blonde hair bouncing on her shoulders, showing me what I couldn't have any more. I could not accept the fact that she had deserted me and had sent me divorce papers without so much as an explanation or an apology. Who the fuck did she think she was? All of those angry, insecure feelings rose up in me and I could feel my pulse beating in my temples. How could she have been screwing about while she was supposedly married to me? So far as I was concerned, the worst thing anyone could be was disloyal and it was especially bad when the disloyal person was a woman.

High on drugs and rage, I tried to run her down; only the lamp-post that the car crashed into saved her life and prevented me from going down for murder. As it was, I was sent to jail for six months for driving without tax or insurance and for having an illegally held gun in the glove compartment of my car. I was very lucky that I did not manage to kill Jane, because that would have made me a murderer, and there is no coming back from that.

I was taken to Ashford Remand Centre. I will never forget the sound of the door as it closed behind me, leaving me in a lonely, barely furnished cell. I was on my own. There was nothing in the room. There was a Bible in the cell and a couple of pieces of basic furniture, but nothing else. It was cold. I was trying to take it all in my stride, but I was absolutely petrified of being on my own. I wanted to cry, but of course there was no way I could let that happen. I remember picking up the Bible and trying to read it, but finding that I could hardly make out anything at all. There were lots of very, very big words and I wasn't even able to figure out most of the small ones. The print was very small and fine and it all seemed to run in together. It was gibberish to me.

I was in that cell on my own for a few weeks, and the boredom and loneliness were such that I actually tried to read, just to pass the time. That was the first time I really tried to get my head around the whole idea of reading. Despite my best efforts, I made no headway whatsoever. It was a relief when I was moved into a cell with someone else, because finally I had someone who could write letters for me to my friends and family, and someone to talk to.

I found those weeks of solitude painfully difficult and I still don't know how I managed to get through them without cracking up. I didn't tell anyone that I was a drug-user because I was scared of the consequences, so I had been going cold turkey on my own. In those days, drug addicts who were detained were put with the nuts and kept in a padded cell, segregated from the rest of the prison population. Having gone through a few days of being on my own, I definitely did not want that.

Like anyone in that situation, I had to try to figure out a way to make ends meet. The prisoners all ate in a big dining room, so that gave me an opportunity to meet people, get to know them and even make friends with some of them. Exercise time was also quite social. But those were the only two opportunities for conversation – I was banged up for about twenty-two hours a day.

I was very lonely, especially as I couldn't read to pass the time, which was what most people did, and I couldn't write letters to my friends on the outside without help. Although I would never have admitted it to anybody, I was scared of everything; the other prisoners, the screws, the system. I was used to having all the drugs I needed at my disposal and without them I felt naked and vulnerable. I had been a big boy on the street, but I was just a small fish in the prison and nobody was impressed by me in the least.

CHAPTER 6

Escalation

I think my grandparents must have hoped my time in prison would act as a kind of wake-up call, but in fact it had little effect on me; I continued with my self-destructive ways.

Shortly after my release, I met another girl and was finally able to forget about Jane. My new girl-friend's name was Christine, and she was wonderful. I met her when I was working on a building site in Raynes Park and living with my grandparents again. Nan had been persuaded to give me another chance, despite all the good advice to the contrary that she'd received from her sons and daughters.

Christine was another blonde. She was very slim and tall, with long legs. She was working on the conveyor belt in a local factory, putting things into boxes. Christine did all she could to keep me on the straight and narrow, and seemed to like and respect me for who I was, and not in spite of it. Thanks to

Christine, I found that I was able to scale back my drug habit quite a bit, although not as much as either of us would have liked.

Still, a degree of drug-taking notwithstanding, things were going well for us, and for the first time in my life I began to have feelings for a girl that approached real, mature love. When I was with Christine, I felt less need to take drugs that would change the way I felt. But of course, when I was with my friends, I took drugs as I always did.

I think I was able to reduce my intake of drugs at this time because, thanks to Christine, I was happier than I had been before. Our relationship was less volatile than the other two I had experienced, and I simply didn't feel the need to use as much as before. Even Nan and Grandad could see that things were better for me and that my life was a lot less unstable than it had been in recent years. We all began to hope that maybe now I would manage to hold it together.

Christine and I were a regular, normal couple. She introduced my mate Brian to a girl called Sophie – the sister of her best friend, Jean. They hit it off, so the four of us hung around in a little gang. Brian and Sophie became serious about their relationship and got engaged. It all felt very stable and, although I was still using drugs heavily, so long as I was with Christine I felt that I had things more or less under control.

Then I found out from her mum that Christine had a condition called Hodgkin's lymphoma, a sort of cancer of the blood, and was going to die. Christine was in her late teens. It all seemed so unfair.

Now that she had been diagnosed, Christine had to go to the Royal Marsden Hospital for blood transfusions on a regular basis. I often took her to the hospital, but I never went in. There was no effective treatment for Christine's condition, but the blood transfusions were supposed to prolong her life and help her to feel a little better. I was desperately worried about her, but mostly for selfish reasons.

Although I thought I loved Christine, I had always had a lot of difficulty in seeing things from others' points of view. When I considered the fact that Christine was going to die, I thought, "What is going to happen to me when Christine is gone?" and "How long is it going to be before I am on my own again?" and "How am I going to manage when the only person who has ever really cared for me disappears?" I can only imagine how Christine must have been battling with fear and anger about what was going to happen to her. So far as I was concerned, it was all about me. I had thought that, finally, I'd found a girl who would stick around, but, instead, this one was going to leave me, too.

Despite the fact that Christine was so ill, we continued seeing each other for about eighteen months before I got in trouble again. This time, I was arrested for shop-breaking, handling stolen goods and taking a car to do the theft in. Although I was working for Tony at the time and making decent money, I still felt that I needed the thrill and the money to buy drugs. When an acquaintance came and asked me if I would steal a car and do the driving for them in a smash-and-grab, I was happy to get back in the driving seat.

I was good at stealing cars; it was easier in those days. Anyone in the business had a big set of keys, and usually you'd find one that would open the door and another that would work in the ignition. If you didn't, it was rarely difficult to hot-wire any vehicle. And it was fun sneaking into someone's drive, breaking into their car and driving off without them even waking up. I didn't care whose car I took. I was happy to take a neighbour's if they had what I was looking for. A good getaway car was something fast and small, like an MG Metro that was easy to manoeuvre and big enough to hold four people.

When it came to the break-ins, we had a system. We'd put on the gloves, dress in black and climb across the rooftops to a shop that we had checked out beforehand, so as to figure out how to get in. We would have found out what sort of lock there was and whether or not there was an alarm. In the winter, as early as nine was late and dark enough for the job. This particular night, we had decided to do a tobacconist's as we would be able to fill our sacks with cigarettes and tobacco and sell the lot on in bulk to a fence who would give us decent money for it. But of course we were caught, despite all the careful planning, and I was looking at some more time behind bars.

After the arrest, I knew that I was facing prison time again and felt that this was more than I could cope with, because I had come perilously close to cracking up the last time. I sat down to think about how I could get out of this situation and, after giving the matter due consideration, decided that if I took a large overdose, enough to kill me or do serious damage, and passed out while somebody rang for an ambulance, then they would not send me to prison. I would be brought to hospital and cared for, so that the overdose did no lasting damage, and I would have demonstrated remorse, so they wouldn't lock me up again. I didn't know anyone else who had carried out a plan like this, but I still felt quite confident that it would work and was not remotely concerned about doing myself any long-term damage.

I went through with it. I took an overdose of Tuinal with alcohol while I was with Christine and asked her to call the ambulance as soon as I fell unconscious so that we could be sure that I wouldn't die or suffer any lasting damage.

"I'm relying on you," I warned her. "Leave it too late, and I'm a goner."

Christine was pale and scared, but she nodded and said that I didn't need to worry, because she would make sure that the ambulance got there on time.

I have always regretted doing this. Christine was a beautiful young woman who was going to die before she had even finished growing up, and yet I was selfish enough to put her in this awful situation. I could have died. I could easily have been left with a permanent disability. And how would Christine have felt then? I have never come to terms with what I did, because by the time I was able to think rationally about it and see just how awful my behaviour had been, it was too late. The stupid plan didn't even work, because when I went to court I was sent away to serve fifteen months in Wormwood Scrubs.

What can I say? Wormwood Scrubs, my new home. What a shithole. This was far worse than the other places I had been detained in. I was surrounded by filth in a small two-man cell that I shared with a traveller called Dave – a Gypsy from Kent of about my age. Dave was in for receiving stolen goods and, like me, had a history of getting into trouble with the law.

Dave and I were two peas in a pod. I thought he was alright, and he returned the compliment. Neither of us could read or write but I was OK at cutting hair and would give Dave haircuts with a razor blade. There were some awful characters in the Scrubs, such as the Hussein brothers, who had been sent down for murder. They had been convicted unanimously, but nobody had ever found the body of their victim, and one of the ways to have a laugh in the Scrubs was to walk past their cell calling out, "Where's the body? Tell us where the body is!" Another notorious killer in the prison had killed a little girl in a wooded area. The press had referred to the crime as the Little Red Riding Hood Murder, and the name had stuck. I was given a job working in the kitchen, which meant that I often found myself serving the child-killer tea and cakes.

Some of the prisoners were so dangerous that they were kept away from the others. In general, there was a very tense atmosphere, and a feeling that the whole thing might explode one day. I worked on the kitchen's hotplate, from where we served all the meals to the inmates. As usual, I managed to work the situation to my advantage and didn't lose any weight while I was in prison.

I can't say that I had any real mates there, but I had lots of acquaintances. Working in the kitchen gave me greater access to baths and showers, which was a good thing, because if you were in the main flow you were lucky to get a bath and a change of clothing once a week. I had always been quite meticulous about tidiness and hygiene and would have hated that. All of my clothes were prison issue and consisted of two white and blue striped shirts, one pair of greys, which were trousers, a grey jacket, two pairs of blue overalls, two pairs of socks, two blue T-shirts and two pairs of white pants, which were like oversize boxer shorts.

We were occasionally allowed to watch films on a portable screen that was set up in one of the rooms at weekends. This gave the prisoners the opportunity to mingle and sort out deals. I earned a lot of tobacco in prison. I became involved in dealing when I was in the Scrubs: sugar, tobacco, food and even drugs. I could arrange for visitors to bring in things in small amounts and get them to me so that I had some currency to deal with. It wasn't hard for my mates to smuggle tiny portions of drugs past the guards. As soon as I got it, I would swallow it or stick it up my bum to be retrieved later; this was the system that everybody used, so my friends knew how to wrap the drugs carefully in plastic so that they would be safe to pass through the digestive system.

Even tiny amounts of drugs were very valuable in prison. Friends brought various things: heroin, dope, cocaine, and more. Another route for drugs to enter the prison was via the inmates who were allowed to work on the outside. In any prison, there are multiple entrance routes for illegal substances.

I wasn't making much money but it was a huge help in making sure that the prison sentence was as comfortable as it could possibly be, and it was a way to pass the time while also raising my social status among the other prisoners. The principles are the same, no matter what you are dealing. On occasions I would want a nice starched shirt for a visit. I would be able to organise this, as well as a decent pair of strides, through my contact in the laundry. Payment was made in tobacco. If, however, we were dealing with something a bit more lucrative, such as drugs, we had money sent to our partners outside and the drugs would be exchanged once information had been received that the money had arrived. Although I was hardly happy during my stay in the Scrubs, I was learning a lot about how the dealing business operated and I was doing quite well.

Despite all the stress that I had put her under, Christine came to visit me throughout my sentence, and we often talked about how one day we would get married and life would be grand. We never discussed the fact that that could never happen, because Christine did not have long to live. In any case, as soon as I came out, I went straight back to my old ways. I started using drugs very heavily, ignoring Christine and generally getting into trouble.

I saw very little of her in her final months, and in fact, she died not that long after I left prison. She was just twenty-two years old when they buried her. Of course, when the news of her death reached me and the reality of how selfish I had been slowly began to sink in, I felt awful. I still feel awful about the way I treated Christine, to this day. I felt so guilty that I could not face attending her funeral. What a great boyfriend. Because I knew that I was a bad person to know, I decided that in future I would avoid nice people. They didn't deserve to have someone like me in their lives. I even drifted away from my old friend Brian.

When I was twenty-one, I served some time in Brixton for stealing cars and some other bits and pieces. I had been involved in "ringing", which is a term that refers to stealing cars, changing their number plates and selling them. I was a petty criminal, so I was remanded and bail was set at £25, which of course I didn't have. Even when I was making decent money through fair means or foul, it was a question of easy come, easy go. As soon as I had a few banknotes in my pocket, I spent them on drugs.

My grandparents were fed up with me at this stage, so rather than asking them to pay the bail, I asked my aunt. Auntie Pat knew that I was taking a lot of drugs and that I was spending time with a lot of very bad characters. But she had always been fond of me, and I was hopeful that she would step up to the plate for me one more time. At that time, I was using a lot of opiates – coke, heroin and Physeptone – as well as some illegally acquired prescription drugs that I had been using for a while, such as Tuinal and mandies. I had discovered that most drugs seemed to do the trick for me, especially if I combined them with alcohol. I wasn't that fussy about what I took and liked the way I felt on just about anything.

Auntie Pat, who had been helping to take care of me since I was a little boy, felt that I needed a shock and that maybe Brixton would frighten me straight. She hoped that this would help to shake me out of my complacency and encourage me to take a long, hard look at my life and where I was heading and make some wiser decisions about what I wanted to do with myself before it was too late. She refused to pay bail, so it was back behind bars for me. I was not happy about it, and felt that she had abandoned me in my hour of need. I railed against her and blamed her for the fact that I had been locked up.

I had served all my previous sentences as a juvenile, but this time I was in with the men. It was completely different from what I'd grown used to. So long as you were a juvenile, there was still the idea that you had some hope of getting your life back on track, and that you weren't so far gone that there was no hope of rehabilitation. But Brixton was a holding ground for hardened criminals. I had thought that the other sentences were bad, but this was much worse. Sexual abuse was very common in prisons – it still is today – and I was a good-looking young man at the time, with long blond hair, and not nearly as tough as I thought I was. In retrospect, I was an ideal victim, and perhaps the authorities should have been more aware of the vulnerable situation I was in. One of the inmates, Steve, who was about ten years older than me, befriended me. He was a figure of respect on the landings and I trusted him. He encouraged me to be banged up in the same cell as him, as he said he would look after me and make sure that nobody bothered me. Of course, what he was really doing was grooming me. And as soon as he got me on my own, he subjected me to some pretty rough sexual abuse.

I got out of that cell as quickly as I could. I spoke to one of the prison officers and told him that Steve was "trying it on with me" and, without saying exactly what had happened, I told the officer that they needed to get me away from that guy as soon as possible. I never wanted to be left on my own with him again. I was moved rapidly into another cell up on the threes (on the third landing).

I have never felt as frightened and betrayed in all my life as I did when I was sexually assaulted. On many levels, I blamed Auntie Pat for what had happened, because I had been given the opportunity to be bailed out, and she had refused to come up with the money, even though I knew she had it and could easily have afforded the relatively small sum. To this day, I have never told her what happened to me while I was in prison, and while of course I know that it was in no way her fault, I do sometimes wonder what my life would have been like if I had never served that sentence and never suffered that sexual assault. There are still times when I am round at Pat's house having a cup of tea and a chat, and suddenly it all comes back to me. In those days, if you were a man and you were sexually abused, you didn't tell anyone, because that sort of thing wasn't supposed to happen to real men, hard men.

Thinking about what happened to me, even after all these years, I often end up with a lump in my throat. I can think about it rationally; ultimately, I was the one who had mucked up and it would never have happened if I had not been involved in crime in the first place. And, of course, the only guilty party involved in the sexual assault was the man who hurt me. No victim of a sexual assault should ever feel that it was because of something they did or didn't do. I know that now. But then, emotionally, I felt as though I had been deserted again and I reacted by becoming determined to be able to take care of myself in every way, no matter what it took. I still hope that one day I will be able to put these feelings completely to rest, because they have stayed with me throughout my whole adult life.

It has often been said that prison is a very good educational centre for anyone who plans to continue a life of crime. Of course, the reality is that prison is mostly full of the least successful criminals, the ones who actually got caught, and one has to wonder how useful their advice is. The *real* experts stay on the outside; they are smart enough to either evade the authorities, or to pay them off. Nonetheless, any aspiring criminal will pick up a few tips by being around prisoners and chatting with them about the things they have done that have worked out, that they have got away with.

Perhaps most of all, prison is a place where identities are moulded. It is where you start to see yourself as belonging permanently on the wrong side of the law, of being external to society and not answerable to its laws, while at the same time knowing that "society" doesn't care about you.

After my brief stay in Brixton and the sexual assault, I became more and more aggressive in my interactions with people on the street. I had always had a short temper, and I had become quite a rough young man in general. I would get aggressive even before I knew there was a reason to defend myself. My reputation as a hard man grew and the more I got involved in criminal situations and carried them off, the more reliable I proved myself to be to the sort of person who needed a chap like me. I was still using drugs, of course, and stealing, and I was always working my way up through the system – essentially as an apprentice in the criminal underworld – and getting to know serious people who were involved in serious business and making big money.

I was still a registered addict at St George's Clinic in Tooting, just around the corner from Wimbledon speedway stadium. This meant that I was getting some help from the health authorities, at least in theory. I would go to St George's to pick up my dexamphetamine time-release capsules; dexamphetamine was a precursor to methadone and was used to treat hardened addicts. I picked up my script weekly and cheerfully combined it with whatever I could get on the street. I also used cocktails of different drugs mixed together. I was off my face most of the time. I wonder now how I even managed to carry out my daily affairs, how I could even function.

Eventually, and not surprisingly, I ended up having another psychotic breakdown because of all the amphetamines I was taking. I presented myself at the clinic where they told me they were stopping my script, because it clearly wasn't working out. They told me to go willingly into hospital or they would section me, because I was not safe to be allowed out on the streets. As I was not in a proper frame of mind to do anything for anyone, I was duly taken in an ambulance from the clinic to Tooting Bec Hospital.

I was totally unstable, virtually paralysed, and went quietly, understanding that there was no other option. I was put on a ward with schizophrenics and patients with other mental illnesses. I was drugged up to the eyeballs and behaved like a zombie. My situation was horrendous. At one stage I developed a condition that is known as "mental lockjaw", which meant that I couldn't open my mouth and believed I couldn't eat or talk. I walked around the hospital corridors for hours on end, not realising where I was, or even who I was. I didn't understand why I was there or what I was doing. I was just an empty shell, wandering around with no purpose. There didn't seem to be any point to anything and I couldn't even summon the initiative to wish that I was dead.

I was medically controlled and heavily sedated, and to this day I can't really remember what went on at the hospital. However, I do remember getting into one fight and the trouble that ensued. The guy in question had had a lobotomy and was sixpence short of a shilling. He was, I believe, a permanent resident at the hospital. Our row had started off as a simple argument about something very minor. He was a big lump of a man and was trying to frighten me. Eventually, we had to be physically separated. Loads of nurses arrived and we were given drugs, separated and told to calm down.

As time went along, I started to feel a bit better, was drugged a little less and had a bit more freedom. One day I remember meeting Kenny while walking around the hospital grounds. Kenny didn't live at the hospital, but he came in regularly to pick up his script from the drug unit. We had chatted and started to get to know each other a little. As I was getting better now, I was allowed to leave the psychiatric unit and wander around the grounds of the hospital, although I was not allowed to go off the site. Life was rather monotonous, so when I saw Kenny I was always happy to spend some time with him. I continued getting better and was allowed to go for longer walks on the common outside the grounds, without supervision. One day I was having my walk when I met Kenny, who had just picked up his script and was in a jovial mood.

"Hey, mate," Kenny said. "Do you want a hit of Physeptone?"

"Why not?" Life was very boring at the hospital, and I was up for anything that would make the day more entertaining.

Kenny told me that he injected the Physeptone for a better buzz and asked me if I would like to try it that way. I had never injected, but it sounded like a good idea, so he set up the works, broke open the ampoule and drew the Physeptone up inside the syringe. He put on a tourniquet, a scarf, at the top of my arm. He slapped my arm until the vein produced itself and then he injected me.

This was the first time I had ever taken drugs intravenously, and I remember it vividly to this day. I was really scared because there was quite a lot of blood coming from my arm, but the rush once the drug entered my blood stream was absolutely unbelievable, like nothing I had ever experienced before. The hit was amazingly fast and powerful. And more than a little frightening. However, it made me feel physically sick, and I slumped to the ground to deal with the overwhelming sensation of nausea. Time stood still and I found myself goofing or drifting off to sleep. It was great, I thought, like a type of magic. It was as if I was under a spell.

Throughout the rest of my stay at the hospital I continued to see Kenny and often bought drugs from him. After he picked up his prescription, we would go over to the common and fix it. Kenny taught me how to do my own fix, and I decided that this was what I would do from now on, as it was so much more effective than anything I had tried before.

Finally, I was discharged. I managed to get a flat opposite the hospital, and before long, I was living with a girlfriend. I met Julie one day when we were both smoking a little dope with some mutual friends. Julie liked the occasional smoke, but she didn't take any other drugs. Although I had been so badly hurt by the failure of my previous relationships, I let down my guard and fell for Julie. She seemed very grounded, and I felt that I could rely on her. We started to see each other and quickly became an item.

Julie was a very caring person, who worked for the Freeman's Catalogue Company. She was an attractive girl, a brunette with pretty features, who could have gone out with just about anyone. I don't know what she saw in me at the time, but maybe she was just looking for a little excitement. Julie moved into my flat with me and after nine or ten months we decided that we would get married. I was managing to work most of the time and, although I was still using drugs, I was reasonably stable. And now I had another white wedding to look forward to! I had no doubt that this time everything was going to go swimmingly. What could possibly go wrong?

Julie and I got married at the Methodist church in Streatham. Although they were very worried about our relationship, and far from happy about Julie's decision to throw in her lot with me, her parents attended the wedding. None of my family turned up. A few of my friends were invited but I can't remember who the best man was. After the ceremony, we went to Julie's mum's for a celebratory buffet.

Julie and I lived in the flat in Tooting, but after about six months Julie left to go back to her parents' house because I was behaving like a nutcase again. Whenever we argued, which was often, I became very aggressive, and she would be afraid that I would lash out and hurt her. Julie hated some of the people that I was hanging out with: minor drug-dealers, petty criminals and generally young men who were up to no good. She realised that in getting involved with me, she had made an awful mistake.

Looking back, I don't blame Julie in the slightest for bailing out of the marriage, but at the time I felt abandoned again and absolutely furious about this betrayal. I worked hard on our relationship and managed to entice her back into my lair. I did this by telling her that I was going to sort myself out and start behaving normally. I promised to get off the drugs and away from bad company. I went back to work at a local building firm and levelled myself out with the drugs. As well as working for the building firm, I was also buying and selling vehicles, mostly legally.

Then I became tempted by the thought of increasing my income and got involved in a sort of scam called the Long Firm. One person would buy a car, and then I would sell it on. Basically, the arrangement was that someone would buy a car by putting down a small deposit, and then there was a brief period of time during which the car was unregistered; this was referred to as "being on the HPI", a list of all the cars that were being bought using a hire-purchase scheme.

I would get the car and go into a sales room, explaining that I was emigrating to Australia and needed to sell the car quickly in order to raise a bit of cash, and that I was prepared to accept a low offer in return for a quick sale. These were top-of-the-range cars, and the car salesman would offer to buy it for maybe half of what it was actually worth. He would know that he was getting a good deal, but assume that I was in a hurry to sell, because I was about to leave the country. He would ask if I had all the paperwork and check if the car was on the HPI register, and of course it wouldn't be yet. I would say, "I don't want a cheque because I'm closing all my accounts so I need the money in cash." I'd get the cash, he would get the car, and by the time he tried to sell it, it would be on the HPI register and there would be a problem. Of course, by this stage I would be long gone. I made quite a bit of money doing this and thought of myself as a success.

This was a great time for music in London, and all the young people followed the latest bands. I loved music and was lucky enough to see Slade at the Temple in Wardour Street. This was in their very early days, when they still had short hair. I'd had to be persuaded to go, because I had seen a picture of the band, and their appearance suggested that it wouldn't be my type of music at all. In the event, they turned out to be a heavy rock band, which was right up my street. I took a lot of amphetamines, smoked a fair bit of dope at the venue and had a fantastic night.

Because drug-taking at rock venues was common, there were often drug raids by the police. They would turn up in uniform, which would give the DJ enough time to warn us about what was going on. We would drop our gear on the floor around us, the police would come in, target a few people and take them away to make an example of them – or fill their targets. As soon as they were gone, the music would start again and we would all be scrabbling on the floor to get our gear back, laughing uproariously.

The police raids were very much part of the fun. That's how it happened at the Slade concert. After the gig I went upstairs, had a couple of amyl nitrates and spent half an hour talking to a parking meter outside the club. As I recall, it was a very serious conversation.

At one stage, I found some legitimate work at the Whisky A Go Go, which was the club above the Temple. The Whisky was a club for soul music and most of the clients were black people of Caribbean descent. Fred, the licensed manager, and I were often the only two white people there. Dope-smoking was the favourite vice of the Temple clients, and as everyone was stoned the whole time there were lots of fights, for one reason or another, usually over some thing stupid that you could be sure nobody would remember the following day.

Despite the scuffles, I liked working at the Temple, and Fred and I became close friends. I had been introduced to him by a girl I had been seeing on the side, and he had sorted me out with a job as a bouncer. I enjoyed listening to the soul music, which was different from the rock I was used to. I found soul quite relaxing, and listening to it gave me a glimpse of a different lifestyle.

Fred was in a band, and sometimes I would work for him as a roadie. At one stage, he did a little singing for a band called Elmer Gantry – his claim to fame – and I worked as roadie for them too, responsible for setting up the stage, sound checks, lights, and so forth. I really enjoyed this work and, being mechanically minded, was quite good at it. It was great fun, and doing something that was both hard work and creative helped me to keep the amount of drugs I was taking down to a more reasonable level than usual.

Afterwards, Fred and I were briefly involved in clothes wholesaling, dealing in the sorts of fashions that the likes of Twiggy and Sandy Shaw were wearing at the time. We were always on the lookout for new ways to make money, and because Fred liked to stay on the right side of the law, we stuck with legal channels. We bought a gowns van, which is a vehicle that has been set up inside to carry clothes on hangers, and we collected high-fashion items from warehouses to sell on to boutiques on the high street. We made good money for a little while before that line of business ran dry and we moved on to something else.

Fred and I also worked backstage in pantomimes. I remember doing a production of Cinderella – starring Dick Emery and Joe Brown – at a theatre in Stratton. I was involved in the lighting: dimming the lights at crucial moments, turning them up and setting up a controlled explosion in a bucket at the climax of the show! Because this was a job that meant having to have your eye on the ball, I wasn't using drugs heavily – just enough to keep me going.

Things were OK for a while. I was making money, and so was Julie. But the more interesting jobs fizzled out and I returned to maintaining a very high level of drug use. I gradually sought out more and more highs and forgot the promises I had made to my wife. Julie and I moved to Croydon into a really luxurious flat. I was earning good money as a jobbing builder for a letting agency, taking care of the maintenance of their properties.

My drug use ebbed and waned. There were weeks when I was more or less in control of the situation. But then there were weeks when I consumed industrial quantities of drugs and treated Julie to an array of dysfunctional, aggressive behaviours. Our domestic bliss was short-lived, as after a couple of months in the new flat, Julie could stand no more of me and left, announcing her attention to arrange a divorce as soon as possible so that she could get on with her life far away from her junkie ex. She left no forwarding address, and I had no way to get in contact with her.

I had lost it all again. It was all Julie's fault, I decided. Stupid cow. Yet again, I had let a woman into my life and she'd messed it all up. Presumably because she was frightened of me, Julie went to live somewhere I could not find her. She was a sensible girl, who was doing the right thing. I couldn't live with myself, so why on earth should I expect anyone else to? Although I was angry and upset, on some level I didn't blame Julie for disappearing and I didn't try to find her or harbour fantasies of revenge, as I had before.

CHAPTER 7

In Business

I remained in south London for a while, although I moved about quite a bit. I lived in Lambeth, Wandsworth, Tooting, Carshalton and Wallington. What all those areas had in common was a dog-eat-dog culture on the streets. You bit or you were bitten.

Although I was gradually getting more deeply involved with the world of drug-dealing, I always had a legitimate job of some kind on the go as well. Despite the fact that he was so disappointed by how I was turning out, my old friend and father figure Tony always had some work for me when I came round and asked him if there was something I could do. I would get into a strop with him once in a while, if I thought that he was making me work too hard or something. We would have an argument and I would storm off saying, "Oh, fuck you, Tony. Stick your job; I don't want it. I'd be better off without you."

Three weeks later, I could always go back and he would welcome me without making any reference to the argument and all my harsh words. I would say, "Hi, Tony, I'll be there at six in the morning, OK?" and he would take me on again, as if nothing had happened at all. One thing I will say for myself is that, despite everything, I was never afraid of hard work and although most of my life was a descent into chaos, when I was working I really put in the time and effort. I have never been the lazy sort.

At this time, I had a desperate need to feel as though I belonged to someone or something. I'd tried – very hard, by my own reckoning – to make things work out in a serious relationship with a woman, and none of that had happened as I planned. I wanted excitement and thrills, but also a gang of my own and the feeling that I fitted in somewhere. Looking back now, I think I was looking for a family and the sort of security and acceptance that I felt I had never had, either in my childhood home or in my marriages.

I was falling deeper and deeper into the world of drug-dealing. It provided me with income and excitement and, increasingly, a feeling of being with the in-group, of belonging, of having an identity. I became wiser to the ways of the business. I had started off selling a little blow, a bit of speed and the occasional bit of coke. At first, I just sold to people whom I knew personally, but now my reputation was growing and I started to sell to people that they knew, and then to friends of friends of friends, and so on. The business grew incrementally, and soon I was the man who was serving people up. This in turn meant that I was meeting progressively bigger dealers all the time.

Because the demand for drugs was growing, I was buying more and more. I started off buying the occasional ounce and graduated from there to pounds. There were people out there who had access to apparently unlimited quantities of drugs, and I liked the fact that I was getting to know them and that I could refer to them by their first names, as if we were equals.

Soon there were huge sums of money passing through my hands. I was the go-to man for all the local petty criminals: people who robbed shops and did hold-ups in banks. Almost all of these people were heavy drug-users, and I didn't care who I sold to, so they came to me for their speed or a bit of blow or coke or maybe to get some downers. I always had a full selection and was proud to be able to offer the punters what they wanted, every single time they came to me for a fix.

My business empire expanded, and so did the amount and range of drugs that I carried. People started to buy from me in larger quantities, and to sell them on to their own customers. I was getting a lot of money and was able to go out and buy progressively greater quantities. My name became well-known in the area, which made me feel wanted and respected. If you wanted twenty pounds of hashish, I was your guy. In those days, that was worth about four grand, which was a heck of a lot of money. It was enough for me to take and invest in more goods and sit back and watch my business grow.

I had a good system. When I had a prospective customer, I would invite them to a meeting and give them a taster of the dope I had to hand. I always made sure that it was the best available. We would end up using a bit of gear together, which established a sense of camaraderie as well as demonstrating the quality of the goods. We might fix it, or snort it. We would do whatever they wanted to try it out and we would have a bit of a laugh together until I saw that they had begun to relax and to trust me.

Then I would say, "Well, you've seen for yourself how good it is. So how many weight would you like?" – "weight" meant a pound. They would say that they wanted ten, or maybe fifteen, and I would tell them to go to a certain address in a week's time, where I would deliver the goods in person and take payment for them on the spot. The deal would usually be carried out in a squat where nobody was living. I moved constantly so that I could not be traced. When the deal actually happened, I would generally sell them one weight of dope and nineteen of almost worthless henna.

This system ensured that I was making huge profits. Increasingly, though, I was ripping off people who were big and important in the drugs world, and that was a very dangerous thing to do. I didn't care. I didn't give a shit. I became reckless. Money was my god, and far better than any woman; certainly, it was more reliable than any of my girlfriends or wives had ever been. And money bought respect, as well as a lot of other great stuff.

On one occasion, I knew a dealer who'd had quite a lot of stuff laid on him by somebody else. I knew that he'd had a delivery because I was knocking up his wife at the time. She had told me when the delivery was coming because she thought that I really cared about her and that she was doing me a favour. She didn't know, of course, that at this stage in my life I was finding it impossible to form an emotional attachment to any woman. I found out that they had ten weight being delivered and where they kept it, so I started cooking up a scheme to get my hands on it in a way that was not going to create too much trouble for me.

In the end, I arranged for four of my mates to go to the house with an old Alsatian that used to go around the place sniffing and pissing indiscriminately. They pretended that they were plain-clothes policemen on the Drugs Squad and that the incontinent Alsatian was a police dog. They banged on the door and shouted to get in at three o'clock in the morning. The sleepy occupants came down to see what was going on, and my friends barged in and started searching the house as though they really were the police. They knew where the stuff was, because I had already told them. They collected it and, still pretending that they were the police, said to the bloke, "Make up your mind, mate. Do you want us to nick you or are we just going to confiscate it?"

They walked out of the house with the drugs and the dog, got into their car and brought the gear to me, because I was the man with the contacts for selling it on. They arrived at my house in high spirits; we skinned up, had a couple of joints and pissed ourselves with laughter, thinking about what we had got away with. We thought it was hilarious. They got their cut, and I made a lot of money. We even gave the dog a treat because we felt he had played his part.

This line of work became my niche, to the extent that when a particular drug was about, people would know which bags belonged to me and where they had come from. I gained a reputation for supplying top-quality gear. The only grass I would supply was top-quality Durban Poison, and the dope was generally Zero Moroccan or Black – dealers came to me expecting the best and I would give it to them, for a price.

As my reputation grew, so did my business network and so did the number of my enemies. I had ripped off a lot of people, and they were understandably very angry about it. At one point, the supplier of one of the men I had stolen from came round to my place in Croydon in broad daylight, kicked the door in and stuck a shooter in my face.

"Give me my fucking gear back or I'll blow your head off!" he said.

I tried to blag my way out of this by telling him I wasn't going to give him any drugs because I didn't know what he was talking about. When I realised that he knew exactly who I was and that I was just telling him a bunch of lies, I changed my tactics.

"Is it really worth it?" I asked him. "If you kill me, you'll end up going to prison for life for a bit of dope."

As you can imagine, I was utterly terrified at this point, but somehow I managed to talk my way out of the situation. I could see the guy with the gun hesitate. "Look," I said. "If you're going to do it, you had better just get on with it. There's really no point in fucking about." I called his bluff.

Although I was scared, it was also exhilarating to know that I'd got one over on him. I could feel my heart rate accelerating. I didn't know what was going to happen next, and I don't think that he did either.

A few minutes later, the guy who had kicked the door down and I were sitting down having a smoke and talking about the business together as though we were old friends. He had realised that he just wasn't going to get the stuff back one way or the other and didn't want to go through with actually killing another human being.

"Look, mate," I said as I lit his second smoke. "You'll just have to swallow it; you lost out on this one, and that's just the way it goes. It could be me the next time, eh?" He swallowed it and I got away scot-free with what I had done. I was elated for several days afterwards, but always wondered when these people would eventually catch up with me.

After that, I gained a reputation as a man who would risk anything. I got some other guys around me and we started to focus on doing deals and finding out where the big money was, so that we could get our hands on it. We were pretty ruthless. We regularly intimidated whoever we had to, in order to get payment.

As I became wealthier, I began to love with a great passion all the things that I could get with money and all the things that money could do for me. I felt as though I would literally do anything for money and all the beautiful treasures that came with it. I started to pay a lot of attention to my image. I bought expensive designer clothes from the King's Road and lots of gold jewellery and dressed up, knowing that I would turn heads when I walked down the street. I looked the part of the successful drug-dealer, with heavy medallions and a flashy car – a red 3.8 Daimler Jaguar with brown leather seats. I felt that I had finally earned the respect of the people I wanted to impress and that at long last I was managing to make a success of my life.

One day I met a new guy, Sparky, who was even more reckless than I was, and who had made great contacts in the drugs business. Sparky took a liking to me and together we started to strike up some deals that involved huge amounts of methamphetamine, which was very sought after in those days. We hooked up with another two blokes, Johnnie and Ricky. We were a gang, but Johnnie was the one with all the serious contacts and the rest of us deferred to him somewhat. He was also the most ruthless of the lot of us.

This was the big time. This, finally, was my chance to make some *real* money and do something with my life that would make people sit up and take notice. Well, I was determined to seize that chance with both hands and give it all I had got! I was part of the firm now.

I was in my element as I moved through my unofficial apprenticeship and progressed up the ladder. I spent a number of years selling drugs and got involved with some very heavy characters across the United Kingdom. At one point, I was making most of my money selling drugs to dealers from Scotland, where there was always huge interest and potential for business. My Scottish contacts would come down to London and arrange a meeting with me, where money and drugs would exchange hands. There was rarely any need for me to actually go north of the border. Basically, what was happening was that huge amounts of drugs were arriving in the country, mostly in south London, where they were distributed to the men at the next rung down from the top, which was the niche that I inhabited together with my colleagues Johnnie, Ricky and Sparky, with Johnnie marginally higher up the pecking order than the rest of us. The drug-dealing fraternity is quite a conservative one in some ways and hierarchies are strictly observed.

I dealt with a bunch that always used to say, when I went to pick up goods, "What are you leaving as a deposit this time? An arm or a leg?" It was said in a jokey way, but really I knew that they were serious.

If I screwed up, they were going to make sure that they hurt me badly enough to satisfy the big fish at the top.

The more serious criminals I knew had a fairly open and regular relationship with the police on their local beat. They had a system whereby they would collaborate with the coppers by throwing them a small dealer now and again so that it looked as though something was being done about the problem on the streets, which meant that the public was kept happy about the police's record in dealing with the junkies whom they saw every day on their way to work, while the serious criminals were able to continue going about their merry way, making money the best way they knew how.

I never personally had anything to do with the police in terms of my drug-dealing career, and fortunately I was too big a dealer to be thrown to them to keep the public happy. Money changed hands, and there was, in all honesty, never a time when at least some of the police force did not know what was going on behind which door and who was making money where. It was well known that some of the people in the Regional Crime Squad became very wealthy by turning a blind eye to the massive amount of drugs being turned over on their patch.

While I never paid any of the police off myself, I once had the strange experience of going to collect a big bag of drugs from a mate's house and walking out of the room, right past a plain-clothes officer who was sitting there without a care in the world. The people who got caught were always the guys peddling a tiny amount of dope on the street, not the more important sellers. I am sure that this is still the case today. Money talks.

By this stage, I had almost completely lost touch with my grandparents. I heard on the grapevine that my grandfather was failing quickly, and when he was on his last legs, I called round to visit and ended up having to take him to the doctor. Nan was frantic and terribly upset. "This is all your fault," she told me. "He's sick with worry about you, after all he has done for you." Grandad died shortly afterwards, and I attended the funeral.

I thought that I was doing the right thing, but my uncles and aunts were all very upset with me because I had long hair, which they felt was disrespectful to the memory of my grandfather. Nan was bereft and she lashed out again, "Look at the state of you," she said. "You didn't even cut your hair and you have the cheek to turn up here when you are the one who put him in that coffin. You should be ashamed of yourself; you're a disgrace."

My grandad had been in his seventies, and he'd had a hard life so, realistically, it was probably his time to die. But although I gave the impression of shrugging them off, Nan's words, spoken in a moment of grief, really hurt. And they have stayed with me always. She may have realised later that it wasn't really my fault that Grandad had died, but in that moment she absolutely meant every word. I took another step back from my family after that, and, following the funeral, my visits home became even less frequent.

Maybe my family members wouldn't have believed me, but the funeral was hard for me. My grandfather had been an awkward old bugger in a lot of ways, but I did love him. I popped into Nan's house every now and again and gave her a few quid, but I never stayed for long. Nan didn't know where the money came from; she didn't ask. And it didn't matter.

Bless her heart, until my grandfather's funeral, she had always believed that, despite everything, her Stevie could do no wrong. When I got in trouble and wound up behind bars, it was always because I was being led astray by somebody else. It was never me; it was the people I was with. Until that day, Nan never challenged me or asked me to explain what I was doing with my life, and why should she have? I was an adult now and it was my responsibility to make my own way through life. She had done the best she could for me. At this point, all of my failings were my own.

In my own world, my arrangement with Johnnie, Sparky and Ricky had become more formal, and we were effectively running a syndicate together. The more drugs I sold, the more money I brought back in. The more the business grew, the more closely entwined our professional and personal lives became. We were all completely nuts, and hardly friends in any normal sense of the word.

As we were making lots of money, we were all using drugs heavily and we were all thoroughly assimilated into the culture of drug dealing, which meant not shying away from violence when it came to getting the money we were owed. It also meant we had no respect for others' property or physical integrity. Each time there was a problem and it was resolved through violence or intimidation, the level of recklessness in our group moved up a notch. Things became incrementally more chaotic.

My business commitments were getting out of hand; I soon had numerous people working for me in different places all over the country. I met them through old-fashioned networking. In those days, the drugs business was much more closely knit than it is today, and it was very much a question of who you knew. Nowadays, dealers tend to buy and sell smaller amounts; in those days, it was a case of fewer people selling more. I was dealing with huge quantities of drugs, and my job was to lay it on the smaller dealers, which meant that I would supply the goods and return for the money a few days later, when they'd had a chance to sell it and make some cash.

As in any business, there were times when I did not receive the money I was owed as quickly or as easily as I liked and needed. This in turn meant that I could not pay the men that I was working for, and as they were very bad news, that meant that I had to be prepared to do what it took to get my money. At this time, I had about three grand going through my hands every week, and I had to make sure that the money continued to flow quite easily. I was earning about a thousand a week for myself, which was a lot of money in the late seventies, but I had an image to keep up and considerable expenses to keep on top of.

I was living in a flat in Croydon, but supplying the trade in Cardiff, so I had to make regular trips – and of course I couldn't go in a small, cheap motor; I went in my white Daimler Sovereign. Cardiff was the central point for the drugs business in Wales in those days, so the suppliers from Carmarthen and other regional towns would know when I was due, and would be there to pick up the supply for their end of the network. The more Cardiff got, the more they wanted. This made me more important, which in turn meant that I was introduced to bigger, more important suppliers and moved up the chain of dealers. Now I could afford to lay huge amounts of drugs on the people beneath me. I had become a man of great influence.

I liked Cardiff and got friendly with a guy called Chrisso, who was married to a lovely woman and had a family and a regular lifestyle. Chrisso was a pretty ordinary bloke who did not use drugs heavily, but he did know some people in the scene. One of his friends was a professionally qualified biochemist who ran a sideline making amphetamines. As I was looking for a new source, I was very interested in meeting him. At the same time, I got to know Chrisso, who adopted an amoral stance on drugs and was generally a very good guy.

One of my main local contacts in Cardiff was an attractive woman called Anne, who was both an addict and a reasonably successful dealer on a fairly small scale. If I was going to bring a large quantity of drugs, Anne would meet the relevant people, I would lay the drugs on them, and then I'd go back and collect the money later on. Anne and I became friendly and developed a rapport. She was good to work with and we hit it off professionally and personally. As I did not have a girlfriend in Cardiff, when I worked there, I stayed at the Hilton Hotel. This was fun, and also part of maintaining my all-important image. When I wasn't working, which was most of the time, I would meet Anne or Chrisso, smoke a few joints and shoot the breeze.

On one occasion, I went back to Cardiff, and my local guy got cocky. He said, "Look, mate, we're not paying you." Basically, he was telling me that they were going to rob me and that he thought there was nothing I could do about it.

I went back to my colleagues in London and told them what was going on.

"Do I have to remind you," Johnnie said, "that when you got the stuff, you were asked if you were leaving an arm or a leg as deposit? If you want to stay in one piece, you'll go down there and you'll get the money." He went upstairs, got a gun and gave it to me. "Go and get the money," he said, "because if you don't, I will be using something like this on you. Because, at the end of the day, people want the money, or they want a body. Don't be stupid, Steve; you don't want that body to be yours. Use this if you have to, or don't, but either way make sure that you don't come back to me empty-handed."

Johnnie was right; I didn't want that body to be mine. I felt a chill as I realised that it wasn't all about the good times, getting cash together and cutting an impressive figure in my swanky clothes.

In the drugs business, if people are ripped off, they won't tolerate it. If it starts to happen on anything like a regular basis, the person in question becomes a laughing stock and loses face in front of everyone they know – as well as losing a lot of money.

I had to go back to the bloke's house with a gun to threaten him and get what I was owed. His name was Rob. Rob, who was married and had a young child, lived with his mother. I knocked on the door of the house and, when Rob answered it, I pointed the gun in his face and said, "I want the three grand you owe me and I want it this afternoon."

"I haven't got it," Rob whimpered.

"You'd better get it," I said. "If you don't fucking get it I'm going to shoot you."

Rob was terrified, obviously. I was scared too. The fact was that I had got myself involved with people who frightened me shitless. I was absolutely petrified and I knew that if I didn't get the money from this guy, they would follow through on every single one of their threats, and more. I didn't want to shoot him and hoped that I would not end up having to do it.

I stayed in Rob's house with his mum, wife and child while he went out to find the money I was after. Rob and his wife were both dealers, and she and her mother must have been terrified having me in their house with a gun. I was far from happy about the situation either, especially because there was a child involved. I just sat in the room staring at all of them. Rob returned to the house after a few hours. He had all my money. I took it from him.

"I won't be fucking dealing with you ever again. Just be grateful I didn't kill you," I told him. I got in my car and fucked off. I drove into Cardiff, continued with the rest of my business and returned to London after a few days. I paid all the money that I owed and was back in good stead with the big boys. I continued doing business with them.

Chapter 8

Serious Trouble

At the height of my career as a dealer, Holland was a source of a lot of the drugs that were coming into England, so it was important to have good contacts there – and I certainly did. While I wasn't at the top of the drugs trade, I was one of a small number of people responsible for bringing all sorts of illicit substances back to Britain and I had acquired some pretty impressive business skills along the way.

The men who occupied the niche above mine were very professional about their dealing. The goods they sold were top notch, 90% pure, and as a result they had a very good reputation; a reputation that they guarded at all costs. They were also known in the business as serious men; people you shouldn't or couldn't cross, because they would do just about anything to take care of their own interests.

Johnnie, who was the main supplier of our group, was known in particular for flying off the handle if money was delivered to him late. He had an obsession with the notion that people were trying to make a fool of him, and whenever he suspected that he was being taken for a ride, he acted like a man possessed. I had a bit of a reputation too; as a matter of fact, at this time my nickname was "Psycho".

One night, I was out with Johnnie and a few others in Crystal Palace. One of Johnnie's contacts lived nearby in an apartment on the top floor of a four-storey building. Johnnie was furious with him, because he was overdue with a payment. He fumed about it all night. Finally, he had a plan: "I'm going to set fire to the building and kill the lot of 'em; that'll show them not to stiff me for money."

"Hang on, Johnnie," I'd said. "There are other people in the building too; you know, people who have nothing to do with you."

"Who the fuck cares?"

It was clear that he didn't care at all, but following our conversation, at least, he decided not to burn the building down.

When Johnnie handed out the goods, he was one of the ones who liked to ask, "Are you leaving me an arm or a leg as a deposit?" Nobody laughed, because Johnnie wasn't joking or exaggerating. If you were overdue with a payment, he might very well turn up and cut off a body part, or maybe two, just to show who was boss. It was rumoured that he had already done exactly that, and more than once.

Because the business that we were involved with was very much illegal, cultivating a close network of contacts was extremely important, and it was sometimes necessary to travel, if not to Amsterdam, then elsewhere. As I became a bigger and bigger player in the trade, I found myself travelling more and more frequently. This in turn meant that I couldn't always be in direct control of what was going on at home, I had to trust my partners and colleagues to cover for me while I was away – and this would soon prove to be a very big problem.

"So," I said to Ricky as I readied myself for my latest trip to Amsterdam, "I'm leaving you to hold the fort. You're up for it, aren't you, mate?"

I was looking forward to the trip. It was about business, of course, but I was also travelling with Judy, one of the girls I was seeing at the time, and I was looking forward to spending some time with her, too. Judy and I didn't have anything serious going on between us, but she was a good-looking bit of stuff, she was fun, and I was quite fond of her. That was about as far as I was prepared to go with any woman, having been burned more times than I cared to think about.

"No problem," said Ricky. "I'm on top of it."

"Don't forget the –"

"Yeah, the delivery in Battersea. Don't worry. I've got everything under control. You just go and have your fun."

"Take my car and do the exchange from that."

"OK, mate. That's not a problem."

Ricky and I had been working together for a while now. We were friends as well as partners, and I liked him. But I didn't realise that Ricky's sense of self-preservation was even less well developed than my own, or that his drug problem was such that he'd begun to lose his grip on reality and forgotten how to assess risk properly – bearing in mind who we were working for.

And I should have known better than to trust Ricky to deal with things while I was away, because we could all see that his behaviour was becoming increasingly erratic. Often, even when we were selling drugs, Ricky would drift off and start fiddling with the other people's safe, trying to get it open or in other ways making us look foolish while we were trying to conduct our business in a serious manner. I knew, but Johnnie didn't, that Ricky was also seeing Johnnie's wife behind his back, which was a seriously bad idea. I didn't realise, however, just how far Ricky was deviating from our business plan. He was out of control.

While I was enjoying Amsterdam with Judy and making useful contacts, Ricky had decided to up the profit factor at home by taking the drugs that we had got from some of the most serious suppliers in the business – the men who provided me with the top-of-the-range drugs that I sold – and cutting them down with glucose until they were only 25% proof.

Our suppliers and, by extension, Ricky and I, were known for providing only very high-quality produce, and our business reputation was based on the fact that the men and women who used our drugs knew that they were getting really good stuff. Once word got out that the goods were actually crap (and that sort of news spread very quickly in our world), it would reflect badly on the guys at the top of the supply chain. It would damage their business and make them lose face. When Ricky hit the streets with the inferior drugs, Johnnie and his pals *had* lost face. And these were men who were serious in more ways than one.

I was in a good mood when I got back from Amsterdam. It was always good to get away, and the trip had gone well. Judy and I had both had a lot of fun. At home in London, I went back to Ricky's place in Croydon, threw my bag on the floor, opened a beer and started to unwind. Ricky was already there, and we chilled out and started to chat. Ricky told me that business had been going well and that he'd made all the deliveries he was supposed to. He didn't mention that he'd been doctoring the goods and keeping the additional profits for himself.

We finished our beers and decided to shoot up some speed. As always, it felt good, and as the effects kicked in, I didn't have a care in the world. I was clearing three or four grand a week, I was young and handsome, I'd just had some time in Amsterdam with my bird and life was sweet. I felt that I had everything sorted out and that I could continue going my merry way through life with plenty of money in my pocket and no shortage of attractive female company.

Then all hell broke loose. Two men, armed with a club hammer and a knife, burst in the door, red-faced and furious.

"We'll be fucking having you," one of them screamed. "You're fucking goners!"

It was Johnnie and his brother-in-law, and I had never seen two angrier men.

"What the fuck?" I shouted as I leapt from my chair. "What the hell is going on here?"

Johnnie charged at me like a mad bull, waving the club hammer above his head and roaring. The beer that I'd been balancing on my lap fell onto the floor, spilling everywhere.

"Try to cheat me, you bastard? I'll fucking show you who's in charge around here!"

Johnnie set to with the club hammer as I held my hands over my face. His brother-in-law wielded his knife wildly, the blade flashing in the electric light. Somehow, Ricky saw a moment of opportunity and fled down the stairs and into the night, leaving me to fend off the attackers as best I could on my own.

In the ensuing bust-up, I ended up with a flesh wound when I was stabbed in my arm and left shoulder. Johnnie had beaten me around the head with the club hammer, splitting it open. Thick, sticky blood was pouring down my face and making it difficult for me to see what was going on. Despite all this,

I managed to get out the open door and run away by blundering through all the back gardens, along the terraced row of houses, knocking over flowerpots and clean laundry and sending the neighbourhood cats screeching in all directions as I went. I didn't stop for a moment to consider how badly injured I was. Fear, adrenaline and the speed that I had shot up shortly before the attack lent the whole scene an air of unreality, and I was acting on sheer instinct.

Finally, I found myself in a garden facing a pair of glass patio doors. I jumped straight through the glass and stood inside the house, blinking stupidly in the light. Blood was pouring from my head and arms and pooling on the lino beneath my feet. I could feel that there were still bits of glass embedded in my flesh and that I was now also bleeding from other multiple wounds.

On some level, I was aware of being in pain, but it didn't bother me particularly. I was much more concerned about getting out of there and getting some distance between me and Johnnie and his gorilla of a brother-in-law.

I knew later that the speed had saved me; if I hadn't been hyped up and fearless because of the drug, I would never have been able to make my escape and they'd have killed me, there and then.

Then again, the speed and all the other drugs I took on a regular basis had also been responsible for getting me into this mess in the first place.

I took a moment to calm down, let myself out the front door and made my way to the hospital to be patched up. While I'd never been the victim of such a serious attack before, going to hospital to have wounds sewn up had become a regular routine for me over the years. Because it was clear that I had been viciously attacked and that I was drugged up to my eyeballs, once I got into hospital, the doctors called the police to interview me. My life wouldn't have been worth anything if I had identified my attackers so, of course, I said nothing. I waited until the attention of the police and the hospital staff was elsewhere and then slipped out. They were obviously going to be looking for the people who had done this to me and no way was I going to tell them who they were because that would be tantamount to signing my own death warrant.

I wasn't feeling great; I was still high, my wounds were hurting, and the fact that I was in a very dangerous situation was beginning to sink in. I had no idea where I was going because my head was all over the place. I couldn't remember the way home, or recognise the area I was in, and passers-by were understandably reluctant to give directions to a man covered in blood, who had just been sewn together and was clearly off his head on drugs. It was difficult to find my way back, but eventually I arrived home at my flat in Tooting.

In the relative safety of home, I began to straighten up. As my head cleared, I realised just how perilous my situation was. I couldn't relax; I kept wondering how long it would be before my door was kicked in to reveal an armed-to-the-teeth Johnnie, ready to kill. I rang some friends and acquaintances and found out that Ricky was OK. When I tracked him down, he was fine, just a little shaken up. He explained what had happened and why my suppliers were so angry.

"What the fuck did you do that for?" I screamed. "You could have had us both killed. And that's not fucking all… as soon as trouble shows up, you clear off and leave me to deal with it on my own. Look at me: I'm in bits. They could've killed me; they still might. And you just… you just…"

This was fucking terrible. This was seriously bad news. I knew that it was time I started to think very hard about what I was going to do next. Ricky didn't seem to be as worried as I was, but I was sure that our lives were both in peril.

I didn't have to think for long. A couple of days later, the phone rang. I picked it up.

"Hello?"

"It's me."

It was Johnnie; he didn't need to identify himself. We both knew that I'd been waiting for his call since he'd set about me with the club hammer.

"What the fuck do you want?"

"I need to see you. Get yourself round to my place, pronto."

"You're fucking joking. A couple of days ago you and your brother-in-law tried to kill me with a hammer and knife and now you want me to come and see you. Do I look like I'm stupid?"

"I want to talk to you and you know there's plenty to talk about."

"You can talk to me over the phone, can't you?"

"I don't want to talk to you on the phone; I want to see you. Get your act together and come over here."

It took me a while to pluck up my courage, but somehow I managed it and went over to Johnnie's place. All the way over there, I had no idea what I would be walking into. My life flashed before my eyes; I wasn't sure I would see tomorrow. But doing what Johnnie told me seemed to be the best of a bad lot of choices.

Johnnie opened the door with a grim expression on his face and showed me in. I was fucking worried.

"So?" I asked with a pathetic show of bravado. "What's this all about?"

But before he had time to answer, I saw Judy sitting in a corner of the room, wide-eyed and terrified. She had been there for several days. She had not been harmed in any way, but nor had she been allowed to leave. She had been questioned over and over again until Johnnie and his friends knew exactly what had happened and who had been responsible for putting shoddy drugs out on the street.

The message Johnnie was giving was loud and clear: I'm prepared to do whatever it takes to keep on top of my empire – even hurt a girl. I tried to look at Judy reassuringly and then turned back to Johnnie.

"If one of us is going to go down, Ricky or me," I thought. "It's not gonna be me."

"What's the score?" I asked. "I don't know what the issue is here; I don't know why you've got a problem with me. We've always got on fine until now."

I knew all about what Ricky had done, but I wasn't about to let on. I needed to be sure that Johnnie was convinced of my innocence.

"The gear that was sold in Battersea – that *you* got from *me* – was cut really badly. It was fucking useless. We never let our stuff out on the street in that sort of condition. I've had everyone coming back to me complaining about it and I can't afford to deal with this sort of problem. I've got a business to run and a reputation to take care of here."

"Hang on, mate," I protested. "That's got nothing to do with me. I didn't do the deal. I couldn't have; I was in Holland at the time."

"Yeah," he said. "I know that now. It's the only reason you're still alive. You can thank *her* for that."

Johnnie gestured towards Judy. She gave me a wan smile, probably more to reassure herself that things were OK than to give any particular message to me.

Now that Johnnie knew that I wasn't the one responsible for the problem, he didn't have a problem with me any more. He even offered me a cup of tea: "You're off the hook, Steve. I know you're OK."

"Your mate Ricky, though," he said. "He's the one with the problem. How dare he mug me off? No one gets one over on me. I'm going to teach him a lesson once and for all. I'm going to kill him, make him sorry he was ever born."

I didn't believe it, and I said so.

"I'm not joking," Johnnie said. "He's in for it for more reasons than one. He's been fucking my wife and he's been cutting my drugs badly. You think I'm the one you should be scared of, but I've got people to answer to as well, and the word from the man at the top is that he wants a body. He wants to show everyone who's boss. Well, there's no way that body's going to be mine, so I've got to come up with the goods. When we went looking for you and Ricky a few days ago, that's what we were doing – going to get a body. The good news for you is that we don't want you as a body any more. We want him. And we're going to get him."

I looked straight into Johnnie's eyes and felt chilled. His irises were enormous and, on this occasion, I felt that it was because of the enormous rage that was possessing him and not because of whatever drugs he might or might not have been on. I had often heard people mouthing off, saying that they were going to kill this person or that person. For the first time, I knew that I was listening to someone who really meant it.

I went straight into self-preservation mode and got out of there as soon as I could. I knew that Johnnie meant it when he said he would kill Ricky, but would it really happen? Maybe Ricky would manage to get away. All I could think about in that moment was keeping myself safe.

Back at my flat, I paced up and down. I didn't want this. I wanted out. I wanted to get away. I considered my options. I was well known in Wales, among other places. In Cardiff, I had a fantastic reputation. Everyone knew that I could get my hands on virtually any type of drug I wanted. I had friends there. Chrisso in particular had always been a good mate. I was fond of Anne, who remained one of the main dealers I supplied. She was pretty messed up, but she had a big heart and I really liked her.

I decided to get a big consignment of drugs, go to Cardiff and disappear. That would give me a nest-egg to start my new life, and the chance to hide out, away from anyone who might want to hurt me. And that was it: I left London, moved to Cardiff and never moved back.

A few days later, I picked up the newspaper to read that Ricky had been murdered; that his was the body that was being thrown to the men at the top. It was a horrible death, too; no nice, clean bullet to the temple. Ricky was killed with a dog choker lead, decapitated, and piled into the boot of Johnnie's car. Johnnie had used this as an opportunity to go around town and lift the lid of his boot to show all the other dealers around Tooting what would happen to them if they ever stepped out of line.

Fortunately for the rest of the dealers, the coppers picked Johnnie up about a week later when they made an inspection of the car and found poor Ricky's remains, still heaped up in the boot and starting to go off.

Johnnie put his hand up to doing the murder straight away. According to what I heard, he seemed almost proud of what actually happened and told anyone who would listen that he had no regrets. It was an easy trial, and Johnnie was sent away to serve time for the murder of his one-time colleague.

For me, Cardiff was sufficiently far away that I was safe there, especially with Johnnie behind bars. No more flashy car and clothes for me. I was determined to keep my head down and stay out of trouble.

I didn't want to end up like Ricky.

CHAPTER 9

Moving out of London

I started to work out a plan to manage and ease the transition from London to Cardiff. I figured out that what I needed to do was get a large quantity of drugs that I could disappear with.

I contacted a big dealer I had used as a supplier on many occasions. I told him that I had some major deals in Scotland and elsewhere that I needed to fulfil, and asked him for a large amount of gear. As I had established a good reputation with him, he was prepared to give it to me on the understanding that he would be paid later. I went to his house, picked up the gear and hired a van; I couldn't use my Jag because it had burst into flames at a service station on the M4 not long before. I had been driving one evening after dark, when I realised that I could smell petrol and noticed that the petrol gauge was going down alarmingly quickly. I pulled into a service station to see what was going on. I got out, went to the boot of the car and opened it up, but I couldn't see anything, as it was so dark.

Clearly not thinking things through very cleverly, I decided to use my cigarette lighter to see what was going on. Of course, it ignited all the fuel that was lying in the boot, singing all my eyelashes and the front of my hair and sending flames high into the air. I started to panic. Not only was I on fire, but the boot was full of gear. I set about taking the gear out of the boot and putting it into the service station rubbish bin, together with a set of scales that I was also carrying. I ran to get assistance. Some of the service station staff put the Jag out with fire extinguishers! I hung around the service station until it was very late and everything had quietened down, and then went and retrieved the gear from the rubbish. I lifted the bonnet of the Jag and extracted some drugs from the air filter and the headlight covers, where I had stashed them. Chrisso, my mate from Cardiff, came to pick me and the car up.

Now without my Jag, I went back to London to pick up the belongings that I could carry and headed for Cardiff. I was welcomed in Cardiff because of the drugs that I was carrying; there was a big drugs scene in the city and there were always plenty of customers. I started my deliveries as soon as I got there, and stayed with some of the dealers.

Cardiff wasn't far, but it was far enough, at least for a while. I cut off all contact with everyone I knew in London and went underground. I was successful enough in this aim that the police didn't know whether I was alive or dead, and there was concern that I might also have been murdered by Johnnie, or else involved in Ricky's death.

So far as I knew, Sparky was still dealing. I didn't want to know about it. A few of my contacts did come looking for me in Cardiff, and turned up in a fancy car asking questions at Chrisso's garage. Thankfully, after looking around a few times, they decided to let it go and I was left alone to get on with my life.

I had brought enough drugs with me to provide me with a basic standard of living, and I also raised a little money selling cars. Whereas in London I had lived the high life with a fancy car and expensive suits, here I released small amounts of drugs slowly into the local market, always on a very small scale, and gradually turned the money I made into a legitimate business buying and selling cars, while also doing the occasional ringer on the side; stealing a car, changing its identity and selling it on. In this way I managed to keep my head above water and pay the bills. I did not enjoy a lavish lifestyle; far from it, it fact. While I had spent a while thinking that I was something of a big shot, now I had to face the cold reality, which was that I was just a small-time dealer like so many others, and all the hard work I had put in didn't amount to anything, after all.

I was lucky in that I had managed to make some friends in Cardiff and wasn't moving into a completely alien environment. My mate Chrisso, in particular, was a life-saver. He took me under his wing and got involved with me in selling and repairing cars, mostly through legal channels. Chrisso would occasionally look the other way if something underhand was going on, but generally he liked things to be done properly and above board, because he was a serious person who didn't like to muck anyone about.

Chrisso became concerned about what I was doing to myself – I was still using drugs very heavily – and tried to look after me. He occasionally took speed and was into smoking dope when he was having some down time, but he didn't go crazy or take so many drugs that he lost control of himself. Chrisso was a cool, calm and collected sort of guy, and I admired the way he used to stay so mellow and not let the little things get him down. I tried to make myself calmer and mellower by switching from coke and speed to using downers like Tuinal and other prescription drugs that I got from my sideline of buying things from people who had broken into chemists, and stolen medication for sale on the black market. So far as I was concerned, this was a major concession to my health and I was being quite sensible.

Chrisso knew that I was never going to deal with an addiction by "treating" it with stolen prescription medication, so he tried to book me into a hospital in nearby Woodchurch to detox. But I wasn't interested, because I didn't think I was doing anything wrong. Although I was still selling coke and doing both speed and coke, I never suffered any repercussions to my physical health, or at least none that I was aware of at the time.

Of course, it wasn't doing my mental health any favours, but such is the nature of the beast that I was totally in denial about that and would have become immensely angry if anyone had suggested that I had any psychological problems at all. When I got angry, I thought that I always had a good reason for it. I was totally in charge of everything, and to hell with anyone who thought otherwise. I felt as strong and healthy as ever and reasoned that that was good enough for me.

About eighteen months after my arrival in Cardiff, the police finally caught up with me. Because I hadn't been claiming any benefits, it had been difficult for them to track me down. I had been put on the missing persons' list. Johnnie was behind bars, but they were still investigating the ins and outs of Ricky's murder and all the events that surrounded it.

In Carshalton, Nan was still living on her own, and because she was the relative I had always had the most to do with, the police thought that I would eventually turn up there. They spent hour after hour sitting outside her house waiting for me to arrive with a few quid for her, as I had always done before. I had maintained a slender line of contact with a few of my aunts and uncles in London and had been receiving increasingly irate messages from them. The situation with the police was causing my grandmother immense stress, and they told me to sort it out.

I set myself up with a solicitor in Cardiff and arranged a meeting with the police at Cardiff Police Headquarters, where I was cautioned and arrested for conspiracy to commit murder. They knew that Johnnie had stabbed me, and had heard that I had been seen making deliveries in Tooting and carrying a gun. Johnnie had told the coppers that he had stabbed me in self-defence, because I had been threatening to shoot him. This was nonsense, of course. Three days of intensive questioning followed, after which it was decided not to charge me. This was a great relief, not least because I knew that I was not to blame for Ricky's untimely demise. In London, Nan moved in with Auntie Pat. She had become too frail to continue living on her own.

By this stage, Anne and I had developed a more serious relationship. We had always got along well, and now things moved up a notch and we became romantically involved. I moved in with Anne and her young daughter Catherine, then aged four. Catherine was a bright little girl and I became very fond of her. Catherine's father wasn't on the scene, so I decided that I would be like a father to her and make sure that she had everything she needed.

Our lives were chaotic in the extreme. I was still dealing, as was Anne, and I was also trying to work at legitimate business and keep the money coming in. We were both using heavily. Our relationship was quite turbulent and we often fell out over money and drugs. Despite our difficult relationship, Anne and I got married a couple of years later: my third marriage. We did the deed at Cardiff Register Office.

All of Anne's family were there, and so were some of my best mates from the area. I liked Anne's parents. Her dad, who had grown up in the Rhondda Valley, a mining area, was quite a hard man who had once had a garage and knew about cars, so we had an interest in common. The Rhondda is a tough place, and people who have grown up there are generally more than able to take care of themselves. Anne's father had done well for himself financially, and the family was comfortably off. Anne's mother was a pleasant, friendly woman. I was happy to be part of their family. They knew that Anne had a big problem with drugs and that I was also a user. Somehow they clung to the hope that together we would be able to overcome our addiction. Perhaps they thought that being married would help us both to sort ourselves out.

I can't remember who the best man at the wedding was, but I know I had one, so I imagine it must have been one of the people I used to take drugs with. Following the ceremony, we had a reception back at our flat. We had a great time with our mates but the day ended in a row. Some people started skinning up and smoking dope in the flat and I was not happy about this – we argued about it, so our first night as a married couple ended on a sour note. Anne and I muddled through married life, but bearing in mind that we were both using and dealing, keeping our relationship up and running was challenging, to say the least.

As things were a lot better for me now, I began to reflect on my life so far. I was twenty-seven, still young, and I had many regrets. Christine was dead, and there was nothing I could do to repair the damage I had done to her.

I also felt guilty about the way I had treated Tony Spooner over the years. Tony had always been there for me, with work and support and advice, and I had thrown it all back in his face. I decided that I would go back to London and thank Tony for all that he had done for me, especially as I felt that my life was under control now and that things were on a more even keel. This was one occasion when I actually managed to follow something through. I travelled to Carshalton with Anne and found Tony, who was still living and working in the area. I explained that my life was much better now than it had been before and said, "Mate, I just wanted to thank you for all you did for me. You were a real support and I am sorry I didn't treat you the way I should have."

I think that Tony had realised how important he was to me, but he seemed embarrassed when I laid it out like that. "I didn't do anything much," he said. "Nothing more than anybody would have done."

"You did, you know," I said, "and I'll never forget it." But I didn't bang on about it, because I could see that I was making him feel uncomfortable.

I am glad now that I got it together enough to actually thank Tony while there was still time, but the reality of the situation was that my life wasn't nearly as organised and good as I thought. I had taken some baby steps towards sorting things out and attempting a recovery, but there was still a very long way to go, and I was still an immature young man.

After seeing Tony, I brought Anne and Catherine to meet Auntie Pat, but we just made a quick visit and left it at that. My feeling was that I was better off out of the family circle, and that they were better off without me, as well. Auntie Pat was kind. She took the visit as a sign that I was moving forward with my life and gave my hand an encouraging squeeze. I didn't let on that I was still using drugs heavily, or that Anne had the same problems as I did.

While we were in London, I decided to take Anne to the St Helier Arms in Carshalton – my old stomping ground and a notorious place for villains and villainy – to prove my credentials. I wanted her to be impressed by how at ease I was with the tough men in my home area. One of the regulars, my former brother-in-law Gary, the hairdresser, had been convicted for murder along with a chap who had also done some work for Tony. These were typical of the clientele of this particular pub. This was a place where strangers were not welcomed. I don't know whether Anne was impressed in the way I had hoped that she would be.

Back in Cardiff, Anne left me on many occasions and went back to live with her mum. But she always came back eventually. I went in and out of detox at Woodchurch Hospital, with Chrisso encouraging me to do what I could to give up taking drugs. My heart wasn't in it. On one occasion when Anne left, I deliberately overdosed on Nembutal because I couldn't stand living the life I was living, and in a rare moment of clarity, realised that I was fucking everything up. I decided that I would be better off dead than alive and that I would be doing everyone else a favour by ending it. I was found on the street and taken to University Hospital, Cardiff. The specialists thought I should see a psychiatrist and referred me to a Dr Callum, who worked at the same hospital.

After my failed attempt at suicide, Anne and I hooked up again, and after a while the inevitable happened: she got pregnant. The baby was planned, or at least not unplanned. We had decided not to use any birth control and just let nature take its course. I was very pleased when Anne told me that there was a baby on the way, because I hoped it would be the thing that would bring us both to our senses and I thought that being a father might help me acquire some stability.

In due course, Anne gave birth to our baby girl, whom we named Michelle. She had made quite a big effort to come off drugs during the pregnancy, and although she didn't manage it, she did reduce her intake considerably. Thankfully, Michelle did not suffer any health consequences as a result of the drugs Anne took. She was perfect. I stayed at home to take care of Catherine while Michelle was being born. When I went into the hospital and the nurses put this tiny scrap of life into my arms, I was blown away: happy and scared at the same time. Catherine was very excited to be a big sister. I thought that I had a proper family at last.

My daughter was beautiful and I loved her, but I felt utterly overwhelmed by the responsibility of fatherhood, despite the fact that I was of an appropriate age to be taking it on. My track record in this area was very poor. I hadn't seen my son Lee since he was a tiny baby; I had lost all contact with his mother and didn't even know where he was. I had sworn to take care of Catherine as though she were my own and had ended up taking an overdose. I had come into her family and married her mother, but we fought a lot of the time and hardly offered Catherine a stable life.

At the same time, I was determined to do things properly now, and I told everyone that I was ready to settle down and be the father of a real family. I was now responsible for two children. Not having had a proper father when I was growing up, I wanted my two little girls to have a better childhood than I had, so I did what I thought was my best to take care of them while making little effort to curtail my drug-taking.

I thought that I was keeping most of the dealing away from our home, but the children often saw me out of my head and doing things like pursuing people down the road while I brandished a machete, uttering threats because they owed me money. Anne was also using drugs heavily, so between the two of us, we actually did an atrocious job of caring for our girls. At one stage, Catherine had to go into care briefly because we weren't looking after her properly.

Catherine had been four when her mother and I got together, and even at that age she had become blasé about the police arriving and turning her mother's house upside down. After Anne and I got married and the family grew, I made a big effort to turn people away from the door, so that at least the children wouldn't have to know too much about what was going on. I should have realised that children always understand a lot more than they are given credit for.

When people knocked at the door and asked to buy drugs, I would stand there menacingly and say, "Fuck off. This is a family home. Don't come to us; we'll come to you." This reduced the number of times the police came to call and turn the house over, but from Anne's point of view, I made her much less independent than she had been before. Before we got together, she had made a reasonably good living selling drugs and hadn't needed to rely on anyone else. By deciding unilaterally that we would clean up our act, I made her very dependent on me, both financially and emotionally. I thought that I was a knight in shining armour, that I was protecting her by taking all the risk. But she didn't quite see it like that.

"I was doing fine before you came along," she would say. "You don't need to take care of me."

"What kind of a mother are you?" I would retort, "if you can't see that it's not right having junkies calling at the door when the children are here?"

All this time, I was extremely dishonest with myself. The law had come to mean nothing to me, but at the same time I had a huge and overwhelming desire to be responsible – to do things properly and well. I wanted to be "normal", but I didn't understand what normal was, although I thought I did. I tried to create a normal environment for my family, but what I did was attempt to mimic something that I believed to be normal life for normal people. It never felt right for me. I wanted to be a good father, the father that I had never had, and I was always talking about it and trying to impress people by telling them what a great dad I was, while not seeing that I would never be a great dad so long as I was taking drugs.

When I had moved in with Anne, the first thing I did was decorate her whole apartment. I thought that this was a nice thing for a normal bloke to do, so I went through the motions and was very proud of the results. As the years passed, I often reminded everyone of what an effort I had gone to. I never got tired of telling people how much under control I had things and how strongly I felt about not letting people come to my home for their fix.

"I'm a serious businessman!" I would preach. "I don't want this crap!" The fact that the business was illegal didn't really come into my head at the time because my main focus was to make a pound and do what I thought I could to give my girls a good life. Alongside selling drugs, I worked in real jobs and, despite the fact that I was using heavily and consistently, I worked for British Steel for a number of years as a crane driver.

I worked nights, and quite enjoyed the job. I obtained my crane driver's certificate. While crane driving, I was in charge of depositing sixty tonnes of molten metal from a huge shed into moulds around which people were working far below me. How I managed not to kill anyone, I do not know. I frequently went to work completely off my head on drugs and reached the end of the day with only hazy memories of what had gone on. Because I had spent most of my life off my head on drugs, it wasn't obvious, or at least people didn't seem to notice. On drugs or not, I enjoyed this job, especially because I was working alongside my mate Chrisso.

I also went to work at another foundry after leaving British Steel, again as a crane driver, where I did a similar job to the one before, but with smaller amounts of molten steel, which was probably just as well.

I liked the fact that I was working with colleagues who were normal men with normal lives who didn't use drugs, and I wanted to be more like them. I was still fixing heroin, but increasingly aware that I never seemed to be able to get my mind into a stable place.

I just wanted to get more in touch with reality, so I finally did something I had not considered before: I went to Dr Callum and asked to be put on a methadone script. This was a very big step for me, and the first time that I had even come close to admitting that there was a problem. I have to admit that methadone did stabilise my life, but only because it made me take illegal drugs less often.

Methadone is a substitute for heroin, the main difference being that it is acquired legally. And while it didn't feel the same as taking heroin, it did dampen my urge to use drugs and helped me to stay in control of things. As I had a responsible and rather dangerous job, I did not tell my employers that I was on a methadone script, reasoning that what they didn't know wouldn't hurt them. And, to be fair, I was doing a good job at work anyway.

Today methadone is given in liquid form, but in those days it was provided as tablets, which I used to crush and draw up through a filter into a syringe and into a vein, rather than taking them orally as I was supposed to. This is a trick that every addict knew and that most engaged in whenever possible. Liquid methadone is very bad for the teeth and today's addicts typically have awful teeth. Fixing methadone this way, however, had the side effect of filling one's arteries with chalk, so I guess it's six of one and half a dozen of the other.

Anne was more into illegally acquired Valium and speed than heroin, and saw no need to get herself put onto a script. She made some attempts to sort herself out, but it can't have been easy, considering that she was living with me, and that I made no bones about fixing up in the kitchen or the living room. For me, the biggest difference between taking methadone and taking illegal drugs was the fact that I was getting it for free and I didn't have to hang around on unsavoury street corners sorting myself out with a dose.

I continued seeing Dr Callum, the psychiatrist I'd met after my suicide attempt. He was a good bloke who looked after me very well within the constraints of the public health system. He tried a lot of approaches to help me get off drugs. He reduced my prescription, but that didn't help at all. He tried hypnotherapy, but was not able to get me to go under, because I was never able to relax enough to relinquish even a little control. Now and again I was arrested on a public disorder charge and would come off the drugs for the couple of days I was in custody, but I was usually back on them five minutes after being released.

Eventually, Dr Callum was left with no apparent option but to maintain me on enough methadone to keep me under control. Most people went to the hospital or clinic once a week to pick up their prescription. I would go on a Thursday, but I was invariably back by the Monday and I'd pick up the same script that I got on Thursday, which meant that I was getting double what I was supposed to.

Dr Callum knew that my prescription would never last a week. I always told him a lie of one sort or another; that someone had stolen my drugs, or whatever. He knew I was lying, and we developed a gentleman's agreement whereby he would leave a fresh prescription for me with his secretary so that I could get an extra dose before the requisite week was up. Although I was using methadone heavily, my life stabilised a lot and I was able to work steadily – which at least meant that I was able to provide for my family.

At one stage I did some industrial painting, which involved painting things like pylons and big chimneys. It was horrendously dangerous, because I was invariably out of my head, swaying about hundreds of feet above the ground. Still, somehow I was always OK and always made it back home again in one piece. Not only that, but I was good at the work and got along pretty well there.

After a while, Anne also stabilised somewhat with the help of legal drugs. She was not on methadone but, I believe, a combination of Valium and antidepressants. These helped her out and made her life a bit less chaotic. But she frequently topped up with illegal drugs because, for whatever reason, she did not feel ready to try to live without that crutch. I didn't need to top up; I was OK with what I had. We would have arguments, sometimes, when Anne dipped into my methadone because she felt that her medications weren't enough for her.

"Stop being so fucking selfish," she would yell. "You're no better than I am; if you were you wouldn't be on the methadone in the first place. And we're a couple. We're supposed to share everything. So just fucking well give me some, OK?"

"At least I am trying to stay in control of it," I would say. "You're a fucking disgrace."

All of our arguments were about drugs or money, and as time passed, we argued more and more frequently. We often neglected to protect the children from these rows, and they had to see and listen to far too many of them. As they got older, Catherine became something of a mother figure to Michelle, at an age when she should still have been playing with her Barbies. She had to cook the dinners and wash the clothes and keep the house under control.

I was a bad friend, too. Chrisso had given me so much and I did nothing to repay him. One day I was driving his twelve-year-old daughter somewhere and stopped the car and left her there while I went into an acquaintance's house to shoot up.

One problem with being on a drug script is that you are very tied down, because you can never go anywhere; you have to stay near the person who is supplying you with the script. If you are taking illegal drugs you have more choice about where you go and what you do because there is always someone who will sell them to you. I began to feel stuck in Cardiff – not that there was anything wrong with it; I just didn't like the feeling that I didn't have any say in the matter.

Inevitably, Anne and I split up.

I received my divorce papers from Anne, citing my unreasonable behaviour, when I was serving a sentence in Cardiff Prison for assaulting three police officers. This, of course, was something that I had done one day when I was off my head on drugs. I got fifteen months, but this was reduced on appeal to nine, as at the time of the arrest I was actually in Woodchurch Hospital, where I was trying to get myself into a safe haven because I had lost it due to alcohol and drugs.

The news was broken to me by my probation officer. When he told me what was about to happen, I went completely mad. I lost control and started to throw myself about and make a scene.

"Calm down, mate," he said. "What's the problem? It's only a piece of paper. You're not any different now from how you were before you got it."

This attempt to comfort me made it even worse. "What do you *mean*, it's only a piece of paper?" I screamed. I had pinned all my hopes for the future on the idea of my becoming a normal, respectable husband and father and now that had all gone down the toilet.

Anne went through with the divorce, bringing my third marriage to a miserable end and leaving two little girls without a father in the house. I felt like shit. I took an overdose in a half-assed attempt at suicide. I honestly did not want to live any more, or I thought I didn't. I had taken a long, hard look at myself and had realised that I did not like what I saw.

"Look at me," I thought. "I'm pushing thirty and I've achieved fuck-all with my life. I'm a fucking joke."

I couldn't understand how things had worked out so badly for me, or why I couldn't stop making all the wrong decisions about every bloody thing. Anything good I had ever done or tried to do had melted and disappeared. I had tried to earn some real money and had ended up living like a dog. I had tried to be a good father and had ended up thrown out of the relationship and abandoning my daughters, leaving them with a junkie for a mother, who couldn't and didn't take care of them as they deserved. I had lied to everyone who had ever cared for me. I had basically cheated my way through life. I didn't like the fact that I knew I was capable of violence. There had been times when I had been walking down the street and a great, hot rage had started to build in me until I felt as though I was going to explode. I had been arrested on a number of occasions for deliberately barging into police officers with every intention of hurting them – just because I hated them – culminating in an arrest for assault. I couldn't even explain *why* I hated the coppers, because I knew on some level that they were just ordinary blokes trying to do a job. I think that maybe, in my head, they represented the authority figures who I felt had always let me down.

Gradually, I became able to think about the divorce more rationally and to realise that yes, the divorce decree was just a piece of paper. It was the end of our marriage, but that didn't mean that Anne and I could not be friends, or that my life was really going to be all that different from before. With time, Anne and I became friends, and we were better at friendship than we had ever been as husband and wife.

In the end, I actually supported Anne when she went to the court office to organise the divorce! This was progress of some sort. In previous relationships, I had never been able to accept it when they ended. At least now I was able to accept Anne's decision and I became quite philosophical about it. I remember telling Anne that the divorce didn't mean much. If we wanted to be together we could be, divorced or not. And if we didn't, then it just wasn't meant to be.

CHAPTER 10

A Difficult Decision

By the time I reached twenty-nine, I had messed up again. Feeling the need for an extra dose one day, I attempted to break into a chemist's in Cardiff to get my hands on some prescription medication that would top up my regular methadone prescription. I made a mess of it and was arrested and remanded in Cardiff Prison. Dr Callum came to see me. He looked at me sadly, disappointed that I had screwed up so badly. But he also saw that he could give me an opportunity to make a real change in my life. Despite what should have been abundant proof to the contrary, Dr Callum continued to insist that I was basically a decent person who still had the capacity to sort his life out.

"Steve," he said. "I can get you out of here, but I can't take you to Woodchurch Hospital for detox, because nobody there is prepared to take you on again. I can, however, take you to Barry Island. It's not a detox unit, it's a psychiatric unit. If you spend some time there, then we can start thinking about sending you to rehab."

"That sounds good," I said glumly, not really meaning it, but realising that there were no other options whatsoever.

The two policemen who had arrested me were in the room as well. One of them turned to me. "Steve," he said. "Listen to what he's saying. Mate, you're not a bad person at heart, and I think you can sort this out like he says. If you decide to do what Dr Callum is suggesting, we'll back you up, put in a word for you when your court case comes up and make sure you get what you need. We'd really like to see you getting your life sorted out."

I didn't trust the coppers to follow through on their word, but I did trust Dr Callum.

"If I get you out on bail," he said, "there've got to be some rules and you are going to follow them."

"OK," I said. "What are the rules?"

"If anyone comes to visit you, we have the right to search them, search their handbag or any of their personal effects."

"That's not a problem for me."

"If you go out anywhere, you'll be accompanied by a nurse."

"Sounds OK. I don't care."

"If you've got a headache, I'm not even going to give you an aspirin for it. I'm giving you nothing. You have got to stay in that hospital until such time as I find you a rehab place to sort you out. Once I find that, we'll organise things between ourselves, but you're not to have anything. Any visitors that come, anything that happens, these are the rules. If you break them, that's it; I'm not going to be able to do anything to help you."

I knew that I had been given one last chance to straighten myself out and I agreed to everything, so I was taken to Sully Hospital on Barry Island to spend some time on a psychiatric ward before my case was heard.

The doctors and nurses at the hospital knew all about where I came from and what my issues were. They knew that they weren't to give me drugs of any kind. For the first time in a very long time, I became completely drug free and this enabled me to start thinking about things with a clear mind. This was a very frightening experience for me; I had never experienced adult life, except through the fog of drugs. But at least I was able to think straight. Little by little, a lot of the truths about my life really started to hit home.

One of the patients at the hospital was a man in his fifties called Mike. Whatever was wrong with him, Mike couldn't sit still. He danced about miserably and continuously, unable to stop moving, even for a second, unless he was asleep. One day, Mike knew that he had a visitor coming. He came to me and said, "Steve, will you do me a favour?"

"Sure," I said. "What do you want?"

"Will you give me a shave? I want to look nice for my visitor." With his perpetual motion, there was no way on earth Mike could have shaved himself.

I agreed, and gave him the shave. I thought to myself, "What's your fucking problem, Steve? You're throwing away your life; you don't want a life. Look at this guy; he's never done anything to hurt anybody, but he can't even shave himself to make himself respectable for his visitor. What the fuck are you doing?"

I started to think about all the things I could do and to realise how lucky I actually was, compared to so many people. Maybe my childhood hadn't been great, but look at all I had: despite everything, I was strong and healthy and I knew how to work hard. I think now that this had been Dr Callum's plan all along. He wanted me to see how much potential I actually had and how fortunate, in many ways, I was.

Not long after I shaved him to receive his visitor, Mike died. He had been in that hospital for years and only got to leave, finally, when he was in a box. Mike was the one who had pulled the short straw. Not me.

After a while, the staff at the hospital began to ask me to help them out with the other patients, as a lot of them tended to wander off and, because they were so ill, were capable of doing almost anything. I always did what the staff asked. I was happy to, really, because otherwise I didn't have very much to occupy my time with. Messed up as I was, I wasn't mentally ill and I didn't need full-time nursing care. I realised that I was quite good at taking care of the patients, many of whom were desperately ill and incapable of caring for themselves on any level. I thought, "Actually, I can look after people; I can do something here."

It felt good to know that my efforts were appreciated and that I was capable of being kind and patient, even when the people who needed care were extremely challenging. I had always had a very short fuse, but that just wasn't going to work in a psychiatric hospital. On one occasion, one of the patients had wandered off and was in danger of falling over the cliff edge into the sea. I went and found the guy, talked to him quietly and managed to bring him back to the hospital in one piece. I felt good about the fact that I had done something useful and maybe even saved a life.

As things started to fall into place in my head, I would take out the photographs of my daughters that I had brought with me to the hospital and break down into tears, feeling awful about having deserted them and having failed so badly at taking care of them when I had the chance. I had thought that I was such a great father, had never lost a chance to tell people all about it, but in fact I had been anything but. Looking at their sweet faces and smiles, I knew that I had sold them very short.

The time at Barry Island was quite lonely. Anne and I had split up, so I didn't see her. And I think that anyone finds out, when they are in prison or hospital, who their real friends are. I had a few real friends, but most of the people I knew were acquaintances, nothing more, and they were already forgetting about me. Chrisso had been a wonderful friend, but I didn't ask him to come. I felt awful about how badly I had repaid everything he had done for me by abusing his trust when he asked me to take care of his little girl.

For the first time, I was able to think clearly. "Why are you throwing all you have away?" I asked myself. "Why do you keep ripping the piss out of anyone who cares for you? Look at the patients here; they can't even begin to look after themselves, and there's you just throwing away your life." I thought about Mike. I said to myself, "Why has he been taken, and not me? I've got a chance at a normal life and I've been throwing it away. I haven't been grateful for all the good things I have and I deserve whatever I get, while poor bloody Mike probably never did anything to hurt anyone. Look at me: I'm a fucking raging animal."

CHAPTER 11

A Chance

Shortly after Mike's death, Dr Callum came to see me at Sully Hospital, saying that he might have found a place for me at the Ley Community – a new rehab-ilitation centre in rural Oxfordshire that was using an approach to treat addicts that was quite different from anything on offer elsewhere. "I think that this might be the place for you, Steve," Dr Callum said.

The Ley Community had been founded by a Dr Mandelbrote, who worked out of the Ashurst Clinic, where I would have to go for an interview to see if I was a suitable candidate for the programme.

I was accompanied to the Ashurst Clinic in Littlemore by one of the nurses, to attend an interview with Dr Mandelbrote, who was the only one who would decide whether or not I would be offered a place at the Ley. Travelling from Wales to Oxford, I remember thinking that this was a big opportunity. I wasn't sure, however, of how successful I would be in fulfilling the admissions criteria. I had been labelled so often that I didn't set my hopes too high. I did not want to be disappointed.

Dr Mandelbrote was a short, stocky, distinguished-looking gentleman with greying hair. He had been hugely influential in the field of mental healthcare, having been one of the first to start unlocking the doors of the mental institutions so that many of the mentally ill could be treated at home and in their communities. He had also done a lot of work with addiction.

I felt very intimidated when I went into the interview room and sat down. It was immediately obvious that there was no way anyone would be able to pull the wool over this man's eyes. It was clear from his body language and posture that Dr Mandelbrote was a strong-willed man who would not let anyone push his boundaries. I was nervous and dying for a cigarette, but smoking during the interview was not allowed.

Dr Mandelbrote asked me a lot of questions about my drug use and life history, and explained a little about the Ley to me. The programme they offered had been developed in New York, and was used in various detox clinics around America. Dr Mandelbrote, in conjunction with Dr Peter Agulnik, had introduced the system to the UK, starting out at Littlemore Psychiatric Hospital before eventually moving to a new location in Yarnton, a small village a few miles outside Oxford, in 1971.

I felt that the interview went on for ages. I was a heavy smoker, and it was stressful not being allowed to smoke during my interview. My fingers kept twitching, and I craved a cigarette more than anything. Eventually, Dr Mandelbrote gave me a piercing look. "I think I'm going to give you a chance," he said. "Go back to the hospital, and we'll be in touch to let you know when your admission date is, and when you should report."

As we made our way back to the hospital, I was really pleased that I had been accepted. I felt for the first time in my life that someone was prepared to take a real risk with me. I knew that this was probably my last chance. I had hit rock-bottom, and if I didn't start to sort things out now, the only way out of the mess was in a coffin. On the other hand, I was very anxious and frightened at the thought of all the upheavals I was going to experience. I would be moving to a new location and meeting a lot of new people and I knew that I would have to make enormous changes. This was serious stuff. Could I really do it, especially as I would be leaving my two children behind? Only time would tell.

Not knowing what to think or expect, I returned to the hospital to wait. I left briefly to attend my court hearing where, of course, I was found guilty of the break-in, having been caught red-handed. The possibility of my going to rehab rather than prison was raised and, true to their word, the police officers who had arrested me put in a good word on my behalf, telling the judge that they felt I had the capacity to pull my life back together. Dr Callum gave the judge a report on me, as well as Dr Mandelbrote's assessment, based on our interview.

It was decided that I would be given what was effectively a final chance to sort myself out. The judge determined that I would have to return to court after three and then six months so that he could read a progress report about how I was doing at rehab. If there were any major setbacks, or I refused to take part in treatment or didn't cooperate, I would be sent to prison to serve my sentence. That was the last thing I wanted. I had decided that it was finally time for me to get my life in order and I hoped that I had it in me to do whatever it took.

After a couple of weeks, I received a letter giving me news of my admission date, the 6th July 1981. I was escorted to the Ley Community by a nurse, and we arrived late afternoon. I walked up the picturesque driveway and was blown away by the surroundings. I hadn't expected a rehab centre to look like this. It was summer and there were lots of flowers in the gardens around the building, which was a large art-deco house that had once been a private home. There was an area for the domestic animals kept at the community, a swimming pool and lots of open space.

I said goodbye to my escort, and then I was on my own. As was Ley policy at the time, when I arrived I was asked to "sit on the bench" and wait to be told what to do. The "bench" is a significant tool at the

Ley. It is a place where residents may be asked to sit when things have got out of hand, they are behaving bizarrely, or even thinking of leaving. It is a place to reflect. The bench is located in the centre of the residents' administrative area. I had all my bags with me and I put them down and sat there quietly until I was received by the staff member on duty, Barry Roberts.

Barry took me into the staff office for a chat, explained what was going to happen and handed me over to two senior residents. I was then taken off to be searched, to see if I was carrying any drugs. They did not find anything; I didn't have anything. This was not always the case, as many addicts arrived with drugs on their person, feeling that they were not ready to give them up just yet.

Following the search, I was taken downstairs into the lounge and introduced to all of the residents, who greeted me warmly. I was freaked out by their attitude. They were all exceedingly strange, I felt, despite the fact that they presented themselves so nicely. I had expected people to be angry or sullen, not kind and supportive. What were they playing at? Was this some sort of a joke?

I had thought that I knew a lot about institutions and rehab, but it didn't take me long to realise that this was a completely different kettle of fish. I had been expecting the process to be difficult and challenging, but I had had no idea just how much that would be the case. From the first day, it felt as though I had, like Alice, gone through a looking-glass into a world in which the usual rules didn't apply. Everything seemed to be crazy; far crazier than in the psychiatric institution that I had just left. I didn't know what the hell was going on here.

The Ley Community was a completely different world, unlike anything that I had ever encountered before. There seemed to be innumerable rules and regulations, far more even than in a prison or hospital, and people were walking around using a vocabulary that was unfamiliar to me, talking about "boundaries" and "issues" and expecting me to calmly accept criticism without getting upset or hot under the collar. As if that was something that had ever happened before.

For the first few weeks, I was looked after constantly. I found out that I was going through what was known as the "safety net period" and that the Ley used a buddy system, which meant that I was never left on my own. During this period there were always a couple of people looking after me. There was one person for Littlemore, which was where I slept, and another for the Ley, where I spent the day. I was told that I could always go to these people for advice or support with anything that came up as I was settling into my new life.

People were friendly, but a little distant, as though I were a large and not necessarily even-tempered dog with which they were suddenly sharing quarters. A few weeks later, when it was apparently deemed that

I had settled in and should be ready to socialise, they started to engage with me more, and while there were plenty of smiles, I soon found out that here, if I behaved like an arsehole, nobody was going to hesitate to let me know all about it in no uncertain terms.

I was used to situations in which people lashed out and shouted when they were annoyed, but here feedback was given in a calm and measured way, even when it wasn't good. I was dubious about the whole arrangement, but I also felt that I'd had something of a breakthrough while I was at the psychiatric hospital, and that I had made up my mind to seize this chance with both hands. I was truly determined not to take drugs ever again and to stay firmly away from my old lifestyle.

As a junior resident, I shared sleeping quarters with other junior residents at a clinic in Littlemore, called the Ley Clinic. There were eight beds in the Ley Clinic, and I was in a room called the Eric Burden Ward with three other residents. It was a tiny room, but addicts travelled light (most of us had divested ourselves of almost all our possessions in the constant search for the next high) so we managed to squeeze in. We returned to the Ley Community during the day.

Our daily routine at the Clinic started with breakfast, which we had to prepare ourselves. Then we were picked up by hospital transport at 8.30 and taken to the Ley Community. A senior resident would drive the community van and return the junior residents to the Eric Burden Ward each night at about 8.30. Each day was intense and very busy and we were generally happy to turn in early.

The bulk of the day-to-day running of the community was coordinated by senior residents – people who had already been in rehab for some time and had made a lot of progress towards being able to achieve their goals. Of course, there were many practical issues that had to be considered, such as laundry, housekeeping, cooking and so forth. Everybody was given tasks to do, and the premises were kept in order by the residents themselves. But far more demanding than any physical work we were expected to engage in were the steps we were all asked to take towards our own rehabilitation.

In a lot of ways, being at the community was like returning to childhood. I was very much told what to do. One of the tasks I was given early on was that of keeping a diary. As I was still almost completely illiterate, someone helped me to write down my feelings. This made me feel very vulnerable. I couldn't write in the diary for myself, so I had to share my thoughts and feelings with a stranger right from the word go. The first entry in my diary read, in someone else's handwriting, "I don't know what it is that I feel and I don't know whether I'll be able to stay here."

In my first few weeks at the Ley, I was told that there was going to be a "GI party". This was a misleading term, and I soon found out that it wasn't a party at all, but that it meant that we were all going to have to clean the whole house from top to bottom. I found myself being ordered around, being told to do things at the double, and that the places I had cleaned were obviously not up to standard. I was certainly not inclined to accept this kind of treatment and told Jerry, the guy who was running the GI, "You're having a fucking laugh, aren't you? I've cleaned this once already are you taking the piss?" I started to square up to Jerry, outraged by his criticisms. Whatever I was, I had never been a slob. I had always taken pride in how tidy and clean my homes were.

I was told off for using bad language and was asked to sit on the bench. What an experience. Who the hell did Jerry think he was? But the amazing thing was, I *did* actually go and sulk on the bench. What was this place doing to me? Why wasn't I standing up for myself?

Although I had undergone detox in the hospital, my mind had not been "detoxed". My body was free of all drugs, but I still felt enormously tempted to use again, because nothing had ever made me feel as good as being high did. Despite this, I was also determined that I would finally do whatever it took to become a normal person, or what I imagined a normal person to be. I decided that if the people in charge asked me to jump, I would say "How high?" and just do it. I already felt completely out of control of my own life and as if I didn't really exist as a person any more. I knew that this was my last chance to sort things out.

When I arrived, it was made clear to me that one of the first things anyone needs to do in order to get better is to surrender, to accept the fact that they have come to change the way they are and the person they have been, because their old way just isn't working out any more. As for me, it was abundantly clear that I did not have the skills or abilities to deal with life in the real world. I was about as competent as a toddler. Why else had I been using drugs for years, if not to provide me with the confidence that I could not find anywhere else? Why else did I start to shout and react violently whenever things did not go my own way? I didn't know when or how to accept others' help, and I didn't know how to recognise which things I might change with assistance from others and which on my own.

The one thing I *did* recognise was how very lucky I had been to be offered this opportunity rather than being sent away to spend some more miserable time behind bars. I knew that there was a lot of urgency in my situation. I was thirty years old and still behaving like an adolescent. But whereas an adolescent still has his whole adult life ahead of him to learn from his mistakes, I had already lived a chunk of my adult life and I hadn't learned anything at all. I knew that if I didn't change, I'd probably kill myself, either deliberately or through the stealth approach that is chronic drug-taking.

As it was, I had abandoned my children. By killing myself, I would be removing any possibility of a place in their lives in the future. I still hoped that one day I would be something like a proper father to my girls. As things stood, now that Anne and I were divorced, the only access I was allowed to the children was strictly supervised. Anne and I had parted on good terms, but because she too was an addict, she was not encouraged to visit. I had permission to see the children for two hours once every six weeks, and I had to travel all the way to Cardiff, a trip of about two hours, to attend these visits. I was driven down by a senior resident, met the girls and played with them, then turned around and came back. There was no question of stopping for a cup of tea or a bite to eat in Cardiff. Because that was where all my old drug-using pals lived, that was where I was at my most vulnerable.

It took me a long time to get my head around the culture of the Ley and how it worked, as it was completely unlike anything else I had ever experienced. I wasn't used to being directly challenged about my behaviour without people getting angry and it all ending in shouting. At the Ley, if I had a smoke and left my dog-ends in the ashtray, someone would come along and ask me, pleasantly but firmly, "Can I make you aware that those are your dog-ends in the ashtray?" If I left my dirty cup on the table they would say, "Can I make you aware that you've left your dirty cup on the table?" The implication was that there was something unacceptable about my behaviour and that I would just have to do something about it, because it was my problem and not that of the person who was annoyed with me. I couldn't, at first, figure out how the hell this was going to help me keep off drugs – I couldn't see the connection and I sometimes just felt belittled by it.

Every second of every day, there was someone around to remind me that my job was to raise the standards of my behaviour to something approaching that of a normal, functional adult. Mostly, the staff involved in the work at the Ley were residents like myself – addicts trying to come clean and turn their lives around. It wasn't at all like being in a prison or hospital where there is a clearly defined "them" and "us". I didn't know what the hell was going on, and I disliked the feeling of being at sea.

I had been at the Ley for about three weeks when it was announced that we would have what was called a marathon group. This was a forty-eight-hour therapy group session during which we would all have time to have everyone focus on us individually; on what we needed, on what we were doing, and on how we were getting along with everybody else. The whole building was blacked out, and lights were kept turned on in all the rooms, so there was no way to tell whether it was day or night. We could go to sleep if we were tired, but had no way of knowing what time it was. It was an immensely disorientating experience.

The purpose of the group was to create a feeling of closeness between residents and staff, and it was a time to openly share the experiences that each resident had been going through. At that particular moment in time, there were about thirty people in the programme, and large rooms had been converted to dormitories to accommodate us. The Community was housed in a large building, but that was still a lot of people living on top of each other with lots of potential for tensions to arise.

The marathon was a draining, exhausting process, involving all the residents and members of staff. When someone's turn came up, all eyes were on them, which was an extremely intense experience. The focus lasted for about half an hour, during which the staff would give a tremendous amount of input in terms of talking to the person in question about where they were with respect to their development, where they were going, and so forth. It was very powerful, and both exhausting and exhilarating.

This was the moment when, for the first time, it was put to me in plain English that the way I presented myself as a father was very far from the truth. In my mind, I had tried to improve my children's lives and had built a good home for them, while everything I actually did had had the opposite effect. I had made their lives much worse than they should have been and had been unreliable and useless.

Hearing this undeniable truth was like having a knife plunged into my heart and twisted around and around, despite the fact that I had come to similar conclusions at the hospital on my own. I remember breaking down in tears, and a number of residents in the marathon could not believe that my tears were heartfelt, as I presented myself as such a big hard bloke. Some of them believed they were crocodile tears and that I was putting on a display to gain some sympathy, which hurt me even more. I had made myself very vulnerable and I needed people to believe in me. But it was one thing just thinking something and another hearing it spoken aloud. It was awful.

But I knew that what they were saying about my experience of being a father was true, and on some level I realised that I had to acknowledge it in order to start moving forward with my life in a meaningful way. When the focus was off me, the staff put on some music and I was given a small memento to remind me of the whole experience. My gift was a little blue elephant that had a white patch on it with red stitches.

At the end of a marathon session, each resident had a record, a piece of music that the others had chosen for them because they felt that it reflected something about them. I remember that Peter's song – Peter was one of my peers at the Community – was *Nowhere Man* by The Beatles. When Peter was told the name of his song he became quite emotional, because that was how he had always felt about himself. Mine was Simon and Garfunkel's *Bridge Over Troubled Water*, which had been chosen for me because – while most of my life had been troubled – the Ley programme would allow me to be looked after in a way that I never had been before.

All residents received the same treatment. After about forty-eight hours, everyone was really tired, including the staff who had prepared food and refreshments throughout the whole session. At this stage, the staff explained that we had all gone through a period of bonding and we were allowed to reflect on the whole event. When the blackout was removed, we found out that it was late afternoon! I shall never forget this powerful experience.

I learned that there were also other therapeutic groups that I was expected to engage with. One of these was called the encounter group. Slip boxes were used. Before an encounter group, residents completed written slips about other residents. For example, someone might write something like: "John, I'm really pissed off with you because you make me feel small in the way you talk to me." Staff and senior residents compiled a slip grid from the comments on all the slips. This determined which residents went into which encounter group and who was Top of the Pops – the person with the most slips.

One function of these encounter groups was to help flush out any of the inevitable problems that emerge when people are living in close proximity, but they also helped us all start to recognise how others live and feel and think, and what is important to them. It was about exchanging a range of different feelings. Hearing how others expressed what they were experiencing on an emotional level also helped to provide us with a new vocabulary for the things that were troubling us.

Sometimes, someone would turn to me and say, "Oh, so how long have you been reacting like that?" and I would reply, "Well, all my life, I suppose." I realised that the origins of my drug-taking lay in my childhood, when I had failed to learn, for one reason or another, how to discuss my vulnerabilities without getting angry and lashing out. These were behavioural traits that I had never even recognised as problematic, or that weren't problematic in the places and situations where I had lived before, but now were entirely unsuitable. If I wanted to stop being a drug addict, I would have to stop behaving in a way that facilitated that lifestyle and set of choices.

It was not easy, shaking off my old habits and attitudes. In the beginning, I attended group meetings, but I didn't really participate or expect anyone to say anything to me. I dreaded the thought of people focusing on me and my problems. I didn't want to know about them, or at least I thought that I didn't. At first, very few residents dared to confront me. I had the knack of being able to look at people in such a way that made it clear they should not dare to speak to me. I was a master of the art of keeping others at a distance. When I did speak, I was abrupt, cold and off-putting. Over the years, I had developed the skill of being intimidating. On the outside, this skill had been intended to keep others at bay. At the Ley, I managed to keep everyone off my case for about sixteen weeks, after which a group session was called about my attitude and how extremely unhelpful I was being.

At this meeting, it was pointed out to me in no uncertain terms that by behaving the way I did, by coming across as aloof and unfriendly and threatening, I was actually robbing myself. By keeping people at distance and refusing to give them the chance to provide me with some potentially very useful insights, I was not allowing myself to grow. My habit of throwing people an intimidating look every now and again stopped them from being honest with me and telling me how I was behaving, and this tendency to put up my defences was getting in the way of my being properly treated.

My natural instinct, when such things were put to me, was to rebel against the rules, to kick against the reins, as I had always done as a child and teenager. My tendency was to distrust everyone's motives and to assume that they could not possibly have a disinterested reason for wishing to engage with me. Often, when someone was telling me something about the way that I was behaving, I turned around and said, "Well, you can bloody well fuck off; if you don't fucking like it, piss off, I don't care about you; I'm not interested in what you think about me." That usually shut them up. But while I thought that I was standing up for myself and my interests, these outbursts left me feeling empty and hollow; feeling like shit, really.

I was not unique in this behaviour. Few people can openly accept that everything or a lot of the things that they've done in their life are wrong, and that they are now supposed to change almost everything about themselves. Regardless of how depressed and dejected we may be, we all have an ego that is hurt when we hear that other people dislike something about us. We all had to learn how to be open enough to accept that kind of criticism.

This was especially true of those of us who had built our whole lives around a need to protect ourselves. We would have to learn how to take apart everything we did and how we did it. We would have to learn that each aspect of our personality and character was connected to every other one, and that in order to truly change, it is not enough to change just one thing. We all had to learn that what we were doing at the Ley was not about simply ceasing to take drugs, while holding onto all our former relationships, our lifestyles and our friends. It meant changing the very lifestyle that had caused us to start taking drugs in the first place. For some of us, this would mean accepting that we could no longer see certain family members and friends, perhaps for ever, and that we had to give up many elements of our lifestyle that we had previously enjoyed and even felt proud of. It meant taking a long, hard look at ourselves and realising that many of the qualities we believed to be essential to who and what we were just had to go.

Throughout the 1980s, AIDS was cutting a swathe through drug-users, and as so many of us had shot up our drugs, this was a big concern. Most of us had shared needles; at some point, we had seen a friend shooting up and said, "Any chance of me borrowing your spike?" We might have given it a rinse under the cold tap, but that was as far as safety precautions usually went.

The thought of having contracted AIDS was terrifying. As it was, lots of the residents had contracted hepatitis from sharing needles. At that time, there was no effective treatment, and most of the people who had contracted AIDS became sick and died very quickly. We were all obliged to be tested for hepatitis, but AIDS testing was optional. I didn't want to know. If I was living under a death sentence, I preferred to remain in blissful ignorance.

As had been agreed by the authorities, I had to return to court in Cardiff for the formal review meeting of my case. I was taken by a couple of senior residents in the community van, and I took with me a written report prepared by my group worker, Barry. I was worried about going to court, but I was even more concerned about going back into the area that I had come from. I was afraid that acquaintances might try to entice me back into my old way of life and get me to start using drugs again. I felt vulnerable. I wondered whether I might have to go back to prison if I did not meet the judge's expectations, and that worried me, too.

I appeared before the stipendiary magistrate who had sentenced me originally. He read the report prepared on me and pronounced himself very pleased with the progress I was making. He felt that it would be good for me to continue to work at the Ley Community and asked me to appear before him again in three months' time. I was really happy with this outcome. I left the court and within minutes was back in the car and on my way to the Ley. I didn't hang around.

In a lot of respects, being at the Ley was immensely hard work, but we also learned to play and experience wonder; for most of us this was something of a revelation. We kept pigs there, and part of my job was to look after them, feed them, clean them out, wash them and generally treat them like royalty. One time I sat up all night waiting for the sow to give birth to a litter of piglets. A couple of my peers and I were there to make sure that when Samantha (named for Sam Fox, the famous Page Three model) gave birth to Eric's piglets (Eric was named after a famous moto-cross world champion), they would be safe. Samantha did not let us down. On my watch, and to everybody's excitement, she produced fourteen little pink piglets. Eric was very proud, too!

Another responsibility I was given was to partici-pate in a "yoghurt watch". Someone was stealing yoghurts from the food shed that was situated in the grounds outside the main building. One of my peers and I were asked to sit up overnight with a lit fire to try and establish who the thief was. He or she never got caught and is still at large. In fact, I think that this is as good a place as any to confess that the yoghurt thief was actually yours truly and as such was never going to be apprehended on my watch.

Despite getting off to a poor start, once I started to engage with it, I realised that although the process offered by the Ley was very difficult, it was a tool that I could work with as I set about making things better. The group sessions and the other encounters helped me recognise that the ways I typically thought and behaved were adolescent and stupid. I even became able to laugh at myself, which is an important step towards healing. The therapy offered at the Ley was often quite playful.

Morning meetings are a good example. Every morning there was a meeting in which we were all brought together to greet each other at the start of the day. We went around the room doing "image breakers". Imagine a big bloke standing in the middle of the room singing "My name is Shirley Temple…" and doing the actions for the curly hair and dancing! These performances were hilarious to those who were watching, but excruciatingly embarrassing to the person doing it. The reason for them was to help us break down our defences and image, and to be more real and be accepted for who we were.

These rituals were therapeutic, but they were also about having childish fun with each other – something a lot of us had never had as children. I remember, aged thirty, spending an afternoon playing commandoes. We all got into the spirit of the game and found ourselves reacting as the children we had once been. "Hey!" I remember saying. "I just shot you and you're still running around. That's not fair!" These games might sound silly, but they made it possible for us all to shed the years of cynicism that we had acquired and, being able to act like children, to start addressing the serious business of growing up properly at last.

My first Christmas at the Ley came around after I had been in the programme for five months. All of the residents were feeling vulnerable at the time; Christmas is a difficult period for anyone who is away from their family, and it's that much worse when the separation is your own fault. I was thinking a lot about my children and what remained of my family. I had not been in touch with my family in London for a very long time.

Despite my trepidation, however, that was the best Christmas that I had ever had. It felt as though we really were just one big family, all looking after each other, exchanging small presents and having lots of fun. It was almost as if we were allowed to be children again. A group of residents cooked a fantastic Christmas dinner and there was more than enough to go around. The formal structure of the Ley was relaxed for a couple of days and most of us were allowed to make phone calls to our loved ones. When we went back to the dorm that night, all we could talk about was what a wonderful day we had had. It was really special.

While we were all learning how to follow rules, we broke them, too. As we residents were not allowed to play cards or be involved in gambling, this type of activity became very attractive and finding the opportunity to play cards was a major preoccupation. My peers and I obtained a pack of cards from Pete. Pete was a Stage Two resident, which meant that he had found a job and started the process of getting ready to move out. At night we played cards in the dorm, with a level of enthusiasm that bordered on obsession. As we were not allowed to carry any money on us whatsoever, our currency of choice was cigarettes and sweets! I wasn't bad at cheating when we were playing poker, so I managed to relieve my peers of several roll-ups and bars of chocolate. The staff never found out, so this was one of the few things I got away with at the Ley.

As the business of therapy continued, another concept that I was introduced to was that of "act as if". Act as if meant learning to behave in a responsible, adult fashion "as if" things were not bothering me, even when they were. This was not about deception, but about learning how to engage in normal, polite, adult conversation, and it is a skill that most people manage to acquire during childhood. The only people who should be able to get away with purely emotional responses to things are toddlers. The rest of us need to learn how to compromise and to express ourselves without screaming and having a tantrum.

There were times when I was angry or upset and wanted to respond to these negative feelings immediately and violently, as I had always done before. Instead, I had to learn to act as if things were OK and didn't matter. I found "act as if" very difficult to come to terms with and it took me a long time to get my head around it. I was always spontaneous and quick to take offence. It was completely alien for me to contain my feelings and I struggled with this challenge.

Everything that I was being taught was about being given a different set of tools, a different way to live, a different way to look at things. It was about allowing people the opportunity to tell me about their feelings regarding what I did and how my actions impacted on the people around me.

As time passed, I gradually got used to my new situation and was able to see the residents coming in after me with fresh eyes. Even after a few months, I had started to change and could see a lot of my old self in the new arrivals. Not everybody who came had been through the process of being detoxed, and some had to come before they had quite finished, or even before they had started. As the Ley Community was about learning to be completely abstinent, they would go through cold turkey. All the residents knew what the newcomers were enduring, as they had been there before, and most offered a lot of comfort, support and encouragement to stick with it. Cold turkey can be awful, but it doesn't last long.

Newcomers were often shocked by what a hard regime the community insisted upon. There was no opt-out clause and there was no medication to make cold turkey any easier. The idea was that it is difficult to make changes in one's life and that anyone trying to start afresh needs to learn to deal with the problems and challenges in their lives in a mature manner and without any props or crutches to make the transition easier.

I remember supporting a male junior resident going through cold turkey at the beginning of his programme. I could relate to what he was going through, as I had been through a similar situation myself in prison, more than once. I reassured him that he could do it. I sat up with him through the night when he was shaking and feeling sick, and reassured him that his yearning to obtain more drugs would gradually diminish. I was positive about what the Ley could offer him and we got through it one day at a time. It was a tremendous feeling, being able to give back, and realising that I could help someone in pain was a major turning point in my own recovery. I felt good about myself on that particular day.

Although the addicts at the Ley were from a wide variety of backgrounds, there was one big thing that we all had in common: we were all grossly selfish. Something had happened in our pasts – different things for different people – that had caused us to grow up with this attitude and behaviour. In some cases, residents were people who had been forced by circumstances to grow up very early and take on adult responsibilities without ever having had an opportunity to be children. This had inevitably had consequences for their emotional development and levels of maturity as adults. Alongside their new responsibilities, they were given this opportunity now.

The Ley used concepts as learning tools. For example, the "onion concept" was at the heart of the programme. Emotional layers were stripped off people in order to reach the centre of the onion, or the real core of the human self. These layers were like the armour that each person had acquired throughout their lives; armour that they intended to protect them from the outside world, but that actually stopped them from ever showing anyone their real selves.

In my case, many of these layers had been formed by taking different drugs and substances that I had used over the years to keep people at a distance, and to get me through a life that I was finding almost impossibly difficult to navigate. Having them removed made me feel very exposed; I was being stripped down and I was made to feel more and more vulnerable. I felt like a turtle prised from its shell. I got all the support I needed, however, from my peers, some of whom had already been through this experience. They looked after me and made me feel safe.

Because of the experiences I'd had at the psychiatric hospital, I had already made some decisions about what I was going to do and had decided to do whatever it took. However, I was in no way prepared for how I would feel when it came to exposing the person I had been, how I felt about my shortcomings and how I had behaved in the past when things were difficult or challenging. I was hugely vulnerable around the issue of my role as a parent.

In my mind, I had always done my best to be a good father and a good partner, and when my relationships had ended, I had invariably been the innocent, wronged party. Exposing the truth of the matter made me feel awful, because it made me realise that I had been behaving fraudulently to myself all this time. The reality was that over and over again I had deserted relationships and abandoned my children. I had to admit, most of all to myself, that this was a real pattern in my life and that far from being a good father, I had consistently run away from my responsibilities and made selfish choices. The first time I had ever tried to be an adult and take care of someone else had actually been in the psychiatric hospital when I had started to care for the other patients.

The longer I stayed at the Ley, the more the programme seemed to be working for both me and the other residents. I could see that we were all making progress. We were a diverse bunch. Coming from a troubled family background was a common denominator for most of us, but not always the case. In some cases, as in mine, factors such as poverty and absent parents were there, but there were some residents who had come from middle-class, privileged backgrounds, but had never been able to live up to their parents' aspirations for them.

Peter, who, I have already mentioned, had been to Eton; you don't get much more privileged than that. His father had wanted him to be a doctor, and although Peter had tried his best to please his dad, he never felt good enough in his eyes and had ended up using drugs and acquiring a major addiction in an attempt to feel better about himself. It is interesting to note that Peter and I actually got on. At the beginning of the programme, I wouldn't have given him the time of day, but as the layers were stripped down from both of us, we found common ground and became very supportive of each other. Perhaps the programme was working. I didn't feel inferior to him and he didn't feel intimidated by me.

CHAPTER 12

Making Progress

As I began to open up to the realities of my life, I realised that the Ley Community offered me role models: people who provided me with examples of where I could end up if I came through the process successfully. These were residents who had been at the Ley for longer than I had, and had not only survived the regime but made real progress. They were on their way towards normal lives and soon they would be leaving the community and making their way through the world on their own.

There were also a number of staff members who were real role models. My key worker, Barry Roberts, was one of them. I felt that Barry actually understood where I was coming from. He seemed genuinely passionate about spending time helping me to untie and untangle those knots within me that I had spent a lifetime creating.

Barry had been a user in his own day and he knew what it was like to be addicted to drugs and to have to give them up. He had managed to better his own situation and move on, and seemed to be the kind of guy who was around for the right reasons. For him, the work he did at the Ley wasn't just a job, but a chance to give all that he had to offer. Although for a long time I retained the tendency to brush off comments and insights that I didn't like, when Barry said something to me, I really listened. Even when I didn't respond straight away, I took it away with me and thought about it in my own time.

There was another man, Paul, who had done the programme and with whom I identified, because he had also been married several times. Paul had a lot of children, and had been a chaotic, erratic person, with devastating results for his family. Yet even he had managed to find it within himself to make the changes he needed for a fresh start.

I always found it easier to take advice and counsel from older people. There were certainly times when younger residents had real insights that I could have found useful, but for whatever reason, I was immensely irritated by a younger person offering advice. I liked the idea of someone older than me, who had seen it all before, and who, I felt, was in a better situation to understand what I was going through.

About a third of the people attending the centre were women. As I had decided that I was never going to become involved with any women ever again, I was exceedingly wary around them, and very reluctant to get to know them. I avoided catching any woman's eye. I had decided that women were, by and large, dangerous and horrible people. So far as I was concerned, I had been trampled on by women all my life, starting with my mother leaving me on my grandparents' doorstep and going through a long series of deceptions and betrayals all the way up to Anne's decision to divorce me.

Although I had made a certain amount of progress, I was disrespectful towards the women generally at the Ley – I ignored them unless they agreed with me and really did not give them the time of day. This was a trust issue; I did not trust women and did not want to engage with them in any way.

This all came to a head one weekend. One of my peers was a woman called Vanessa, who was a coordinator for the work we all did. Whenever I felt that Vanessa was wrong about something, which was most of the time, I challenged her authority in no uncertain terms. One weekend, it was my turn to organise the clean-up of the house in the morning. One of my peers, Ronnie, was helping out. We organised the clean-up and did, we felt, an admirable job. Then Vanessa told us to address the residents because she felt that our work hadn't been done to a high enough standard. Addressing the residents was one of the rituals of the Ley Community whenever anyone hadn't stepped up to the mark. We didn't agree with Vanessa's assessment of the situation, so we totally ignored her request.

"You're talking a load of bollocks," I told Vanessa. "You don't know what you're on about."

Unfortunately for me, Sue, a staff member, was on duty that weekend. She pulled Ronnie and me to one side and gave us a talking-to.

"Steve," she said. "You really need to take a good, hard look at your attitude towards women. You've got a lot of work to do there and you are not going to get better until you've got it sorted out."

"You don't know what the fuck you're talking about," I told her. This landed me in hot water, and Ronnie, too.

"I think you had better both go and sit on the bench," Sue said.

I rolled my eyes at Ronnie. So far as I was concerned, all Sue was doing was confirming everything I thought about women. Bossy, demanding, unreliable women. Who needed them? Resentfully, Ronnie and I went and sat on the bench. About fifteen minutes later, Sue came to tell us that we were on contract for the weekend. This was a tool used to enable people to spend some time away from their peers within the community so that they could think about their behaviour and the consequences of it. A contract was supposed to be an opportunity, not a punishment. When a resident was on contract, they were given a boiler suit to wear and were not to speak or make eye contact with any member of the community apart from one person who was allocated to them to provide support.

Excluded from community life, I was sent to clean out the coal shed at the Ley. This meant taking all of the coal out of the large shed and depositing it outside on the ground, and then scrubbing the walls of the empty shed with a brush until it was deemed to be clean. It was a particularly pointless exercise, I thought. The work took about four hours. I was then told to put all the coal back into the shed.

"How the fuck is *this* supposed to help me change my life?" I wondered. "Why is it so important for me to clean bathrooms, wash dishes, respond to bells and adhere to the structure? And what's the bloody coal shed got to do with anything?"

I had never realised how important such tasks were to people in the "real world". But, despite myself, I came to learn that I needed to be part of the team, to have some self-respect, to play my part and to have a purpose. I couldn't expect everything to come to me and be done for me. It was up to me to take responsibility for myself.

The weekend passed, and on Monday morning Ronnie and I were put back on the bench. Now we would be addressed in a general meeting, which was a meeting of the full community. Ronnie and I would have to stand in front of the community while we were addressed about our behaviour. I stood in front of the community and was told that I was a useless father, that I was intimidating, that I was disrespectful towards women and that none of this would be tolerated. I did not say anything. Ronnie turned to me.

"We don't have to put up with this bollocks, Steve," he said. "I'm out of here. Are you coming?"

For a moment I considered leaving, but I realised I needed to be at the Ley no matter how hard it was.

"I'm not going anywhere," I told Ronnie. Ronnie walked away.

I stayed put as I was addressed by the staff, who questioned my ability to make the changes that were required. This made me furious. Come what may, I was determined that I was going to prove them wrong. I would do this programme and I would succeed. Brian, the director at the time, said, "Steve, I'm not sure that you are going to be able to do this. It's going to be hard and I'm not sure you've got it in you to make it work." This made me even more determined.

I was put on contract in overalls in the kitchen washing up dishes from six in the morning until ten at night, seven days a week. I was on contract for the next six weeks. At the end of this six-week period, I was put onto a hard works contract which included a special exercise that I was really not looking forward to – working with the women. The thought of having to interact with my female peers made me feel very insecure and vulnerable. I presumed that they would take advantage of the situation and treat me badly, because I knew that they didn't like the way I behaved. I completed my contract and was put to work.

I had to take part in trust exercises with the women. This was very frightening. In one I was encircled by all of the women and blindfolded. I was then told to cross my arms across my chest and to fall backwards. The women were to catch and save me. They did. In another one I was blindfolded and told where to walk by a couple of women residents. I had to trust that they would keep me safe and not let me harm myself. Again, they did do this.

Then there was an encounter group in which the women confronted me about my behaviour and let me know how it affected them. I had to put myself in their shoes and learn how to see myself and my behaviour from their point of view. I didn't like the fact that they were frightened of me and intimidated by me, and that they didn't trust me. This was the first time I genuinely realised how I actually affected women around me. I realised that I wanted and needed to change, very much.

These groups and trust games went on for about three weeks while I still worked on contract in the gardens. They did not let up, and I was not given the opportunity to fall by the wayside. They worked really hard with me and during the process my relationships with the women gradually began to improve. I felt relieved that there was some trust between us now and I knew that I had to continue to work on that.

The process also brought into play my issues of abandonment with respect to my mother leaving me as a baby. I had to come up with some answers in my head as to what might be the truth about her leaving me. I had to question my father's part in this.

Was it his fault that she didn't stay? Maybe she had genuinely felt that she had no alternative. With the women supporting me, I worked through this issue.

It is no exaggeration to say that this was an amazing experience. Eventually, I learned to accept that all women, like all men, are different, and that I had been involved in the failure of all my relationships just as much as my partners – if not more. The reality was that if I had picked the wrong partners, I had only myself to blame. In the case of my marriage to Anne, as I had been an addict with another addict as a partner, conflict had been inevitable. I learned that my relationships with women had been about a combination of old-fashioned lust and the desire to find someone to look after me and be the mother I had never had. Above all, I started being able to forgive my mother for having abandoned me as a baby.

Looking back, I can see that this was the moment when I really started to get better. I will always regret that so many of the women in my life, from Nan to my wives, girlfriends and daughters, had to pay a high price for my inability to deal with this for so many years.

Thinking hard about my mother, I realised that my father, who was a jealous, possessive, violent alcoholic, must have been impossible to live with. Doreen Parker left me with Nan and Grandad, who had already raised a large family, and were good people. She did the best she could.

Not long after coming off contract, I had to return to court in Cardiff once more. Again, this caused me some concern, because Cardiff had been my home for so long. I knew a lot of people there and I was still afraid that this would make it difficult for me to go back to the Ley. I was before the same stipendiary magistrate again. He read the latest report, was very impressed with my progress and said that he would allow me to finish the programme, concluding that there was no need for me to appear in front of him again. It was fantastic to be going back to the Ley in the knowledge that I was there because I wanted to be, rather than because of an order from the courts.

Because the Ley was all about helping people to grow up, I was expected to change not just emotionally but also to acquire the normal trappings of adult life. I was expected to open a bank account. This was a big hurdle for me. I couldn't read or write, so what was the point of my having an account? How was it going to work? Would I be able to go into the bank and say to my banker, "Can you write a cheque out for me?" I was sure that the man behind the counter would say, "We can't do that, sir, you need to do that yourself." Then I would have to say, "No, can't you understand? I'm asking you to write it out for me because I can't do it myself." I didn't feel ready to deal with that kind of embarrassment. However, as usual, the reality of opening an account was actually less stressful than I had imagined.

At the Ley, I was finally able to tackle the illiteracy that had been playing its role in holding me back over the years. It was suggested that I was probably dyslexic and that it was likely that this was why I hadn't made much progress at school, all those years before. In those days, there was little support for dyslexic students, especially children who came from poorer families in which relatives were not in a position to offer much support.

I started to attend evening classes for dyslexia in Oxford. It was tough at first, but eventually the penny dropped and I started to make progress quite quickly. The teacher who ran the literacy class was amazing. She helped me to break the task of learning how to read and write into manageable pieces. She made it clear that not being able to read and write wasn't the huge deal that I thought it was; that it was a situation that a lot of people were in. Illiteracy turned out not to be the terrifying demon I had always seen it to be. From being sure that I would fail, I was delighted to find that, with each class and each reading experience, it became progressively easier.

Because I had not been able to write home since entering the programme, I was desperately anxious to write a letter to Anne, Catherine and Michelle. It was a wonderful day when that actually happened. That was the first letter that I had ever written anybody. I told the girls how well I was doing and asked them if everything was OK in their lives.

It was a real weight off my shoulders when I realised that I had failed to learn at school because I was dyslexic, and not because I was stupid. It had never been a question of my being incapable, but of the right sort of help not being provided to me when I was still a child. The more I read and wrote, the easier it became. I learned that reading and writing were largely about memory; about keeping things focused and to the forefront of the brain. Whereas I had only ever picked up a newspaper to hide behind when I felt that people were looking at me more closely than I liked, finally I was able to actually read the paper. For some reason, I found it more comfortable to read it starting from the back, but that didn't seem to be a problem, so that's what I did.

I had opened a bank account under a degree of duress, but as I grew more confident about my writing skills, I became determined that I would write my own cheques. First of all, I just put the figures and the date in, and signed my name. I could write "cash" but if I wanted to write "one hundred and fifty pounds", that was beyond me, so I would hand the cheque to the person I was buying from and ask them to fill in the rest. Little by little, I didn't need help any more.

With my new reading and writing skills, I was very proud to be given the job of admin manager at the community. This was a very responsible position. The admin manager was responsible for organising the administration department, which included taking messages on the telephone and logging the whereabouts of all the residents. It involved a lot of writing.

Although I was dyslexic and had only just learned how to read, I was the one who had actually asked for the job. I wanted to push myself to the limit. In the end, I actually managed the department quite well because I used what I had and I organised things so that I was working with others. It was up to me to find the tools I needed for the job, and doing so was an important lesson for me. I learned that there was no need for me to beat myself up about the things that I wasn't able to do; that, instead, I should just find other ways to do them.

As my confidence grew, I found that, through the programme, I was able to get involved in things that before I would never have imagined possible. I volunteered and was accepted to help run the local youth club. The director of the Ley felt strongly that the residents should be involved with the village we were living in. The residents in Yarnton had been understandably anxious about having a bunch of addicts living in their area; there's a tendency for people to think that there is something radically wrong with people who take drugs and that they are extremely dangerous, but the community had been widely accepted by the village. The director's feeling was that we should give as much back to the village as we could. So he started up a youth club and asked me, now a senior resident, to get involved.

The local police officer helped too, and in the end, there was a little group of us running the club. At first, I did not know how to engage with the young people, who were aged between eleven and sixteen. But the more time I spent with them, the better our relationship became. They would come to me for chats and ask for advice. This made me feel a great sense of responsibility and I was determined to do my best for them. Strangely enough, the parents in the village never got involved in helping with the youth club, and I could never understand why, as the kids were so engaging and it felt wonderful to be part of their lives, even in a small way.

As my time at the Ley neared its end, I went into what was known as Stage Two, which meant that I was still living at the Ley, while working for a wage outside. I found a job working as a lorry-fitter for a haulage company for three days a week in the trading estate next door. There were no secrets between my new employer and me. He knew, obviously, that I had been through rehab and that I was a person with a long history of unreliability. Because of that, Alan told me that he would start me out on just three days a week until he felt happy enough with my performance to take me on full-time. After I had been working for Alan for about four weeks, he turned to me one day and said, "Mate, you've got a full-time job." We shook hands and I was absolutely delighted.

I became enormously fond of Alan, a much older man who had a son about the same age as me. He had taken a gamble on me, and I rewarded that by working as hard as I could. Alan was a kind soul. I remember one day I was working on the floor when Alan came in and went mad.

"What the bloody hell are you doing lying on that floor?" he said. "Steve, that's just not on. That's not OK."

"What's the problem?" I asked, afraid that I had done something wrong.

"Don't stay there; you'll end up catching pneumonia. Look; there's a bloody laying-down board there – get on that board and take care of yourself."

At first, I just worked on things like changing tyres, fixing the lorries and doing bits and pieces around the workshop. But after a few months, I was given the responsibility of opening the yard in the morning and closing it at the end of the day as well as taking messages on the phone. It felt great, being able to write those messages down. I realised that it didn't matter if I wasn't able to spell every single word; I could always ask the person on the line how to spell the difficult ones. That was what adapting was all about.

Early in the programme, the staff at the Ley had found out about my interest in motorbikes, and I had rebuilt an MZ, a German brand, for one of them. Now that I had reached the second stage of the programme and was actually in employment, I managed to save enough money to buy a blue 125 Suzuki. I stripped it down and turned it into a bit of a trials bike and took to riding it round the back of the community where there were some big fields.

After a while, some of the residents, who had been watching me performing tricks on the bike, decided to build a small ramp and lie in front of it to see how many people I could clear on my bike. The ramp was duly built, I took a couple of practice runs, and then some of the residents started to lie in front of the ramp for my jump. I knew I could do it so I wasn't remotely worried about the outcome, although I can't say the same for the people lying on the ground!

I revved up and cleared the ramp and the residents, no problem. Flushed with success, they decided that my next task would be to jump my bike through a ring of fire. We cobbled together a long, thin piece of metal turned into a ring shape, which was then bound with straw, coated in petrol and set alight. The ring was placed firmly in the ground. Once again, I revved up and jumped clear through it. The residents and staff all cheered and a good time was had by all. To this day, I still have a photograph of me jumping over the residents on my bike.

CHAPTER 13

A Fresh Start

I was still attending adult literacy classes when something marvellous happened. I always took the bus to the class, which was held in a college in Oxford. Various other courses were also held there, and I got to know by sight people who were using the bus to attend one course or another. One day, I saw a familiar face at the bus stop and started to chat to the young woman, who introduced herself as Alison. We hit it off, and from then on, every time I saw her on the bus on a Wednesday afternoon, I sat down beside her and we had a chat.

She was gorgeous, and although we just talked on the bus, I felt that I was getting to know her, and that this was a woman with whom I could actually be friends. I decided that I wanted to ask her out, but I was afraid of what she would say when she realised what sort of person I was. One day, I plucked up my courage enough to say, "Would you like to go out for a meal with me?" To my delight, she said "Yes".

Because I was still at the Ley, I had to go through formal channels and ask the people in charge if it was OK to take someone out for a meal. I got the thumbs-up and we went out, but I couldn't drink any alcohol.

"I'm curious," Alison said. "Why don't you drink?"

I took a deep breath and decided to tell her the truth. "Well," I said, "the reason I don't have a drink is because I'm not allowed to drink at the moment. I'm actually in rehab, because I was a drug addict. So I'm not allowed to use anything like that."

Alison just looked at me and smiled.

When I had asked Alison out, all I'd had in mind was making a friend, someone with whom I could maybe go out for a meal once or twice a week. She had always been so friendly on the bus that I had felt that I would like to get to know her. But as time passed, our relationship began to grow into something deeper. Visitors were welcome at the community, so she came to visit me, and found out what it was all about. When I realised that I had told Alison the truth about myself, all the dirty secrets, and that she still liked me, I knew that I would have to do all I could to keep her.

Before I knew it, the time had come for me to move from the Ley into a place of my own. I decided that I would live in nearby Cowley, but I didn't have enough money for the deposit on the flat.

"How much money do you want, Steve?" Alan asked. I was £180 short. "No problem," he said. "I'll ring my wife up and she'll bring it over for you."

"But I don't have it to give it back to you, Alan," I protested. "I don't want to see you out of pocket."

"Give it back to me when you can," he said. "I'll stop it out of your wages."

Maybe for Alan lending me the money was no big deal, but for me it was tremendous, and I knew that his faith in me to repay it was all because of the changes that I had managed to make in my life. Perhaps, I realised, I wasn't the person that I felt I was. Perhaps I could actually be someone else. Someone better.

When I moved out of the Ley and into my own place, Alison decided that she would come to live with me. At first, I had my reservations about this, considering how poorly my previous relationships had all worked out, but we decided to give it a go and moved in together. We stayed in Cowley for about nine months, before moving to a small cottage, just across the road from the Ley, in Yarnton. I continued working with Alan until he sold up and moved on, and then found work at another business in the village, Charlett's Tyres, as a tyre-fitter. I fitted into village life quickly, having got to know a lot of the locals through my work at the youth club.

It was around this time that I got involved in motocross – all-terrain motorbike riding. This hobby turned out to be a life-saver, and it helped keep me on the straight and narrow. Through motocross, I got to know lots of people and travelled all over the country.

It started when Alison's boss, John, brought me to some race meetings and got me involved as a spectator and a marshal. I had loved bikes since childhood and I knew I would really take to racing. I saved up for my first bike, a 440 Maico. This particular bike was one of my biggest mistakes. I spent most of my time on my arse! I knew nothing about these machines and, obviously, I learned the hard way. Although I had many tumbles, I loved the sport and continued working hard to learn how to get good at it.

The first meeting I ever went to as a rider was in Garsington, a small village on the outskirts of Oxford. It was in a ploughed potato field, and taking off from the gate with another thirty riders was quite frightening, especially as I didn't have a clue how to corner on the bike or take the bumps that presented themselves to me. It all looks very easy from the side-lines, but when you are actually on the bike, it's a different story. I would continue to persevere in the sport for the next thirty years. Motocross was also an adrenaline-fuelled way of ridding myself of the aggression that I carried with me most of my life, and the rush I got from competing was better than any hit I had ever experienced from taking drugs.

I travelled all over the country and even as far as Holland, Belgium and France. Once, when I was racing in Locken in Holland, I had a horrendous experience when my handlebars snapped in half going round a corner at speed. I lost control and came off the bike. I didn't realise that I had broken my hand until I got back to England. What was really annoying was that I had been about to have my road motorcycle test in England. I decided to strap up my broken hand and take the test anyway. I took it in Aylesbury and passed. Only afterwards did I find out that, although I had no recollection of it, I had already passed my test years before. I had sat it when I was using, and all memory of it had vanished in a haze of drugs.

After I had spent a few years in the outside world and had remained on the straight and narrow, a member of staff, Paul, let me know that there was a vacancy for a group worker coming up at the Ley Community and that he wanted me to apply for it. I had been working as a tyre fitter for three years and quite liked the work, but I was very excited to think of the possibility of being able to give something back to the community that had literally given me every-thing. I had some assistance in completing the appli-cation form and handed it in at the Ley.

I was shortlisted and attended a formal interview. I was interviewed by Brian, Paul and Peter, who were all people whom I had known since my time at the Ley as a resident. I found this experience extremely daunting. It is much harder to be interviewed by people who know you, and these three knew me very well, having seen me during some of my deepest, darkest moments. I answered their questions as best

I could. One of the people that I was up against was an ex-resident called Louise. Louise got the job. I was terribly disappointed to have to continue tyre-fitting, although I didn't mind the work. Despite the setback, I kept up my relationship with the community and continued popping in and out, doing odd jobs and working at the local youth club.

About a year later, I was told that there was another group worker position going at the Ley. I wasn't sure whether I wanted to go for it, because I didn't want to be disappointed again. I was OK where I was and I didn't want to rock the boat. However, a number of people close to the Ley kept advising me to go for the job and reassured me that I would be good at it. I decided to submit my application again. The interview went well and, after a short wait, Brian rang to tell me that the job was mine. I was very excited but wondered whether I had taken on something that was completely out of my depth. Only time would tell.

Being a group worker was very unlike being a resident or being someone who just popped in and out giving advice on occasions. I was now in a position to make life or death decisions about people. In those days, the regime for staff at the Ley was less rigid than it is today. There were hardly any rules and regulations, so I fitted in quite well. But there was still a lot for me to learn. It was very different, being on the other side of the treatment package. My position made me feel very responsible, and I had to think carefully about any decisions I made and get used to working closely with the team around me.

One birthday, two of the former residents, Brian and Pat, decided that they were going to go out and buy me a present. I knew that something was up when I found them peering at the Yellow Pages. I took a look at the page in question and decided that they must be shopping for parts for a car. I was very excited. Instead, Brian and Pat had been shopping for poultry. Later that day, they drove up the long Ley driveway, parked their car and came into my office with a big sealed sack and a big grin on each of their faces.

"There's your present. Happy birthday," they said. I opened the sack and an enormous big black turkey jumped out of it, frightening the life out of me. Brian and Pat burst into a rousing chorus of "*Happy Birthday to You*".

"What the heck am I going to do with a turkey?" I wondered. Fortunately, we have a really large aviary at the Ley, and Steve the turkey moved in with the peacocks and the rest of the birds. I was delighted. My close friends often refer to me by my nickname, "Turkey", to this day.

Bonfire night was always a highlight of the calendar at the Ley Community. The staff played games with the residents, pretending to set fire to the bonfire ahead of time and raising their territorial hackles. A huge bonfire was erected a couple of weeks before bonfire night and was added to by the residents to make it even larger. We told the residents stories, encouraging them to think that there was someone out there who was going to come in the middle of the night and set fire to their bonfire.

On one occasion, a wardrobe was taken off the bonfire and laid down in the middle of the lawn with a staff member inside. A trickle of petrol was dribbled from some bushes to about five feet before the wardrobe. The petrol trail was set alight, while activities were going on in the lounge. When this happened, there was an immediate reaction – all of the current residents rushed out of the main house to see what was going on. One of them noted that the wardrobe was not on the fire and decided, along with a couple of his peers, to move it. All of a sudden the wardrobe door flew open and out popped Barry. As you can imagine, this caused quite a stir!

* * *

Nan died in her mid-eighties after a long life filled with hard work. I had seen her a couple of times since sorting myself out, and she knew that I had finally managed to turn my life around, but we had not been in contact much. After graduating from the Ley, I had decided to wait for a while before renewing contact with my family in London. We had all been through false hopes before, when I had said that I was going to sort myself out, only for me to disappoint everyone again. I didn't want to let them down.

Somebody rang me to let me know that Nan had died and that the funeral was over. My aunts and uncles had had a family meeting, and it had been decided that it was better that I didn't go. Too much water had passed under the bridge, and there were too many difficult memories. I think that, in some ways, they were trying to protect me from emotions that would have been difficult for me to deal with.

After three years of being involved with the Ley in a professional capacity, I applied for a senior group worker position. I must have been doing something right, because I got the job. I felt ecstatic. It seemed that the boy from Lambeth had come a long way. What I actually sang in my head when I was offered the job was, "The working class can kiss my arse, I've got the foreman's job at last!"

At around the same time, although I had never thought that I would settle down and buy a house, Alison and I did exactly that. We'd been together ten years when she proposed to me on 29th February, a leap year. I said that I did not want to get married.

"Why fix it if it isn't broken?" I asked. "We're perfectly happy as we are."

"Will we *ever* get married?" Alison wanted to know. "I'd like to get married."

"Sure," I said. "The next leap year." I put my promise out of my mind and forgot all about it.

The December before the next leap year, Alison reminded me of my pledge. Although I had been married three times before, my relationship with

Alison was the longest I had ever had – longer, in fact, than all my previous relationships put together.

We went ahead and organised the wedding which took place at Bicester Methodist Church. The week before, about twenty-five friends and I descended on the Centurion pub for my stag night. It was quite low key; I was drinking again, so we just had a few beers and a great laugh. I had renewed more regular contact with my family in London. Now that I had something to be proud of – a good job, a partner and my own house – I felt more confident that I wouldn't let them down again. Uncle Albie had already come to visit us a few times with his wife Janet. They'd had a family, and the children were getting big. It was great that, after all these years, we still shared a passion for motorbikes. He admired my bikes and was very interested in my stories about motocross. Auntie Pat and Uncle Pip came, too. I had told everyone that I had finally sorted things out in my life. But I think that I needed for them to actually come and see me in my new home so that they could be reassured that this time I was telling the truth and not just spinning them a pack of lies as I had done so many times before. I felt that they needed to see the physical evidence that I wasn't bullshitting them any more. I really had grown up and changed.

On the day of the wedding, I went in the pub before the ceremony and had a few large brandies to settle my nerves. I hoped this would be the last time I would walk down the aisle. I had asked a mate,

Ian, to be my best man and I had invited my family from London to join us for the special day. We held our reception at the Centurion. A marquee had been erected in the garden, and the wedding dinner was curry, baked potatoes and a vegetarian option.

Lots of my family attended, and all of Alison's family were there; we had about a hundred and twenty guests, and a fabulous time. During my using days, when I thought that I had so many friends and knew so many people, I would have considered myself very lucky to be able to organise a gathering with twenty.

As senior group worker, one of my responsibilities was to teach group workers. I gave presentations on residents and talked about difficulties that particular staff might have with specific residents. We would go through these issues as a team, and between us we came up with ideas and different opinions as to how the goals could be achieved with the particular person. I was also very involved in parenting groups. From having been the man who abandoned his own children, I had learned a great deal about parenting. The addicts who come to the Ley typically have huge problems being good parents and equally huge difficulties accepting this fact. I often hear addicts telling me about what great parents they are. That was just what I always used to say, too.

Before long, I was promoted to assistant programme director. I was given a lot more autonomy to make decisions about running the community. I had just been introduced to Chris Lambrianou, who was a former member of the Kray gang and had recently been released from prison. I was asked to have some input into helping Chris re-establish himself. Chris was on licence at the time and was being supported by Mike Howard, the Ley's liaison probation officer. As you can imagine, providing support was no easy task, because Chris had just spent fifteen years in prison and clearly had a lot of issues that needed to be worked through. He wasn't a resident of the Ley, but came here to get support and did voluntary work for us, which eventually led to him working at the Ley full-time.

On one occasion, I asked Chris to go into Bullingdon Prison to talk to the "lifers". Chris was very reluctant to do this and we ended up having a face-to-face argument about what my expectations were. Eventually, Chris gave in, after considering my request carefully. This was a very big move for him as he was not the sort of character to give in easily. When Chris returned from the speaking engagement, he told me that he had realised how important it was for him to go and share his experiences with these people. He shared some hope with them for the future. Chris actually felt very good about what he had done and recognised where I was coming from.

This was not the only time Chris and I came head to head. But one thing is for sure: we have always been there for each other. Chris no longer works for us, but occasionally pops in to see me to catch up on old times. He often reminds me of the strokes that he used to pull and didn't get away with! Once, he had gone to London to pick someone up from court. On his return to the Ley, he handed me a parking ticket, with the expectation that the Ley was going to pay it. I asked him a couple of questions. One was, "Did the Ley park the car there?" When Chris responded that no, it hadn't, I asked him whose responsibility it was. Chris laughed and said, "Mine". The Ley did not reimburse him for his parking ticket. He was a trier, but very loyal, and to this day remains one of the few friends I completely trust.

I was facilitating the admissions meeting one day when a case presented itself to me. A man called Steve, who was in his late forties, was living under the stairwell in a multi-storey car park. He was an alcoholic and in very poor health. I was advised by the Ley's local GP that taking Steve into the programme would be a huge risk, because he doubted that he was healthy enough to complete it successfully.

Steve came to visit the Ley on a day placement for assessment. He looked much older than his years and was very empty, with little hope for the future. Following the assessment, and against advice, I made the decision to offer him a bed there and then. It was obvious to me that Steve would not last very long left to his own devices, and I felt that I could not stand by and allow this to happen. You would think that Steve would have been really grateful to the Ley for this intervention, but that wasn't the case. As he had made life difficult for himself on the outside, he made it difficult for himself and those around him while at the Ley. He was one of the most argumentative residents I have ever worked with.

But there is a happy ending to this story: Steve successfully completed the programme and, although ill health prevents him from working full-time, he engages with the Ley doing voluntary work and is a real asset to the community. I'm very proud of him.

My job as assistant programme director was not all about success. There were many disappointments along the way, too. Some residents left prematurely with the intention of going back to their old ways and some of them died as a result. When this happened, it was a stark reminder of what could have happened to me had I not had the opportunity to do the Ley programme and see it through to the end.

Although the Ley has always had more male than female residents, there are plenty of success stories among our women, too. I clearly remember Rachel when she first arrived at the Ley. She was highly strung and very wary of what was going to happen to her. We had our yearly sports day about a week after she arrived. It was a beautiful, hot summer day. Residents were preparing the field so that we could have sack races, egg-and-spoon races and all the other fun games that go on during sports day.

Rachel insisted on wearing her huge, furry winter coat throughout the day. I think she enjoyed the attention that she received because of it. Little did she know that she would soon have the attention of the whole community. She was on the veranda with her peers, when all of a sudden she collapsed. All the residents started shouting for attention. An ambulance was called and Rachel was taken to hospital. We were later notified that there was absolutely nothing wrong with her, apart from attention-seeking. Had she taken her coat off when requested, we need not have called on the good nature of our emergency services. Rachel, who successfully completed the programme, is now a trained teacher, and we both laugh about her histrionics to this day!

I had been assistant programme director for about seven years when the position of programme director became available. I applied for the post and was interviewed once again by Dr Mandelbrote, who was the chair of the Board of Trustees. I was successful and became programme director of the Ley Community. The boy from Lambeth really had done good! Thinking about it now, I feel that this was genuinely an amazing achievement. Having gone from where I started to being the programme director makes me feel really proud. I know that everyone really does deserve a second chance, because I am proof of this.

Alison and I had been together for a long time when she accidentally fell pregnant. This was not something I was prepared for. I had told Alison right from the beginning that I did not want children; I had been a useless father and didn't want to mess anyone else's life up. I did not want to abandon any more children. At the time, Alison had told me that she understood this and that she would not try to force the issue.

When Alison told me about the pregnancy, I'm afraid that she did not get the reaction she wanted. I was very scared of what the future might hold and how my life would be affected. I still doubted my abilities as a parent. However, I gradually came to terms with it as the pregnancy progressed and now I can see that it was the best thing that could have happened to me. Daniel was born and he has given me the opportunity to finally be the good parent I wanted to be. He has really been a wonderful gift.

Chapter 14

Rehab

Rehab has always been a difficult field to be in, and the depressing reality is that it's never been more difficult than it is today, despite the fact that we know more about addiction, on paper, than ever before. Successive governments like to be seen to be doing something to keep the junkies off the streets. Junkies have been parked on methadone for years, allowing them no real chance of full recovery, but at great expense to you, the taxpayer. Sending people to state-funded rehabilitation can look, from the outside, like an easy option.

Many people who don't understand addiction often say, "Why aren't these good-for-nothings being *punished*? Why are we paying to send scumbags like them to what amount to glorified holiday camps? Why can't we just lock them up and throw away the key? They're just criminals, aren't they? The type of people you'd cross the road to avoid; they should be sterilised so as to prevent them from breeding. They're a drain on society. They're not like you and me. They are *bad.*"

The fact is, though, that drug addiction is a problem that affects people from all walks of life. It's true that many of these people become involved in crime to fund their habit. It's also true that a lot of them are good, intelligent women and men with a lot to contribute, so long as they are given the help they need to change their lives. Personally – and sure, I am also speaking from my own experience – I believe that everyone deserves a second chance.

But if you want to talk numbers, it might be surprising to learn that keeping someone in rehabilitation for a year actually costs considerably *less* than keeping that same person in prison for a year. And while few addicts come off drugs permanently as a result of a spell in prison – indeed, plenty of people get their introduction to hard drugs behind bars – effective residential rehabilitation offers a chance for people to change their lives immeasurably and to become productive citizens, good parents – and taxpayers. Pillars of society.

In my darker moments, I often wonder if successive governments have had any interest in curing addicts, or if they have been more concerned with building up their own drugs empire, with the social workers, doctors and other caregivers taken on as hapless frontline dealers. Originally, methadone was supposed to be a temporary crutch, designed to ease addicts away from drug-taking and back into normal life. But, more often than not, it's not like that at all. It is not uncommon for people to stay on methadone for more than ten years. And, until recently, all people were put onto methadone scripts with no exit strategy at all; how mad is that? I've had personal experience of taking methadone, and while at the time it stabilised my life and made it easier for me to function more normally, it didn't do anything to change the root problems and behaviours that were behind my drug-taking and chaotic behaviour.

Drug addicts will always find a way to get the high that they crave, whether they wind up grinding their legal methadone to a powder and injecting it for the edgier sensation you get from doing that, or selling their legal high on the street so as to get their hands on the fix that they like better. Methadone, like the heroin it replaces, is very damaging to health and well-being. I've seen the same experience replicated over and over again in the lives of the many people who have presented themselves to the Ley Community, desperate for a fresh start. Methadone might look like a good idea, and it has a role in short-term treatment, but any more than that and it's like a hamster's exercise wheel. You might get onto it and feel like your life is finally going somewhere, but you're really just running in endless circles.

Drug-taking is just one small element of a much bigger picture of a lifestyle that needs to be fundamentally altered so that a person can grow up. In

Britain today, the state plays an enabling role that goes way beyond providing addicts with constant access to methadone programmes. While I am very much in favour of a welfare state that protects all its citizens, there is something wrong with a system that pays people a basic living wage without challenging them or expecting them to step up to the plate and behave like the adults they are supposed to be. The answer lies not in withdrawing benefits, but in asking and expecting people to give back to their society in the form of responsible work that benefits their community and themselves.

Today, I engage with people who are starting on their journey of recovery. As I did, they struggle with accepting criticism and advice. They will tell people to fuck off, that they are not interested, that they couldn't give a shit what others feel about them, or what they feel about others. The closer the advice or insight is to the bone, the more it hurts. Recovering addicts can take a long time to learn that this feedback from their counsellors and other professionals and, above all, from their peers, may be hurtful, but that it is essential to their development and to their maturation as autonomous adults. Once they have begun to accept that they can't get better on their own, they are already on their way. By the time they are able to look back at their old selves and have a little laugh about how stupid and immature they were, healing is taking place.

What we offer at the Ley Community is essentially a second chance to grow up, to relearn or learn for the first time about taking responsibility. All the residents that complete the Ley programme go into full-time employment when they leave, often being employed for the first time, paying taxes and no longer being a burden on society. Rehabilitation is not a quick fix, and in my opinion, anyone who tells you that they can give an entrenched addict a fresh start in as little as six or twelve weeks is either hopelessly optimistic or lying. Any addict engaged in that kind of programme will not be leaving to take up employment and live independently, but will end up living on benefits in supported housing.

In the area of addiction and rehabilitation, there have been marked changes since I started work – many of them far from helpful. Increasingly, addicts come from families that not only do not help them as they go through rehabilitation, but may actively hinder them, even going so far as buying drugs for their addicted children. This makes it very difficult for those of us working in the area of rehabilitation to help. We need the people who come to the Ley Community to understand that they will have to make enormous changes in their lives. When there are parents or other family members back home communicating the message, "Look, give it a go, but if it's too difficult for you, just come back to us and we'll see you right," there is always a back door and an escape route from a journey that is often painful, and that can seem to be too great a challenge to take on. Many parents and other family members feel guilty, as though it is their fault that their loved one is addicted, and they do what they can to make their lives easier, not realising that they may still be caring for their overgrown adolescent, when he or she is middle-aged and they themselves are old. There is a great need for education in this area, and for spreading the message that there are times when it is actually more positive, more helpful, to stand back and leave the work of rehabilitation to professionals and to the addicts themselves.

The situation for women addicts has also become more complex than it was when I entered rehab in 1979. When I did my programme, there were many more women in rehab than there are now. Currently, women with children are riddled with guilt and also know that there is a real risk that their children will be removed permanently from their care if they admit that they have a problem. Knowing this, they have become less likely to attend rehab at all. This is a real disappointment to me as I know that the family work we carry out at the Ley with women residents enables them to re-engage with their children and become good parents in the long term.

Attending rehab will never work for everyone, but it works for a lot of people. The Ley programme is about changing attitude and behaviour, and it is about recovery.

As a final note, to anyone who remains unconvinced of the real importance of meaningful rehabilitation in our society, I would like to reiterate this: it's cheaper. At the time of writing, it costs about £35,000 to keep someone in prison for a year. The chances of that person ever holding down a good job, or a respectable position in society are minimal. About 60% of the people in prison are there for crimes relating to alcohol and/or drugs. It costs £25,000 to keep someone in our residential rehab for twelve months, and, if they stick with the programme and see it through, they are more likely than not to return that sum to society tenfold – and much less likely to reoffend. They have been given the chance to grow up, and they have taken it. I'm not naïve. There are always going to be some people who cannot or, more likely, will not be helped. But even if we can save a third of those otherwise in jail for drug offences, just think of what a difference we have made in the world!

I have a little story for you. I have a friend who, for many years, didn't realise that I had been a drug addict in a former life. When I told him, he didn't want to believe me, because the respectable, mature man he knows didn't fit with his image of a junkie. As a matter of fact, my friend had just finished telling me that all drug addicts were leeches and that if it was up to him – he being a former military man who doesn't like to mince his words – he would put them all up against a wall and shoot them.

Shortly afterwards, my friend had a spell of ill-health, and wasn't able to carry out some work he needed to get done in his garden. I arranged for a few of our residents to go over and attend to the job. They did it really well, had a chat with my friend and made their way back to the Ley Community.

"They did a great job, those chaps," John said. "So who are they?"

"Oh, them?" I replied. "They're some of the residents at the community. They're some of our addicts."

"Addicts? But they were alright, weren't they?"

They *were* alright. They had been given a second chance at life and they were seizing it with both hands. Because, with the right help, addicts can and do recover. Recovery is a reality.

CHAPTER 15

And then …

When I moved away from London, I didn't care if I never saw my father again. I had bumped into him at Uncle Pip's funeral, when he passed away far too young. I went up and said hello to Dad, and we exchanged small talk for a little while, but we didn't speak for long. I think that he was too ashamed to talk to me. About twenty years later, I got in touch with Theresa, who was still with him after all that time.

"Your dad's sick," she said. "He's in hospital. He's on his last legs."

After speaking with Theresa, I put the phone down and went to think about what I had been told. My father had never done much for me. On balance, he had contributed to making my life and especially my childhood much more difficult than it should have been. But I realised now that I could move away from that; that I could forgive and forget. I really didn't want him to die thinking that he had been a bastard and nothing else. Whatever he had done, no doubt there were things in his own life that had led to him turning out the way he did.

I also realised that while I had always been very good at blaming my father for things, I had long ago reached the stage where I had to take some more responsibility for myself, and not just put everything on him. Even if he hadn't been a good father, maybe I could have done more to keep our relationship alive later on, too.

So I went to see him in hospital so that we could say goodbye. I made a big effort to be pleasant to him and we were able to talk. He was in and out of hospital for a while, and on one occasion I was the one to take him home. I am glad to say that I saw him on the day he died and helped to arrange his funeral.

On the day Dad died, I went to sit with him for a few minutes on his own. He looked very small, lying in the bed. I felt that I needed to have a quiet word with him, even though he was gone. Nobody heard me – or certainly he didn't – but at least I said it.

Afterwards, I thought about my mother again. Although I had largely managed to forgive her, thanks to the Ley, I had always felt that in abandoning me she had sent me along the wrong path and bore a lot of responsibility for how things had worked out. But at this stage, I had to accept that I didn't know the full story and never would. Two things had enabled me to finally change my attitude towards women. One was gradually becoming able to forgive my mother, and the other was working with the women in the programme while I was a resident and with women staff members over the years. I am pleased to say that I have never looked back.

Latterly, I have had to fight a lot of battles, many of which result from my own behaviour in the past. When you are an addict, you don't ever consider the damage that you might be doing to yourself physically. I know I didn't. Little did I know that the time bombs were ticking inside me, and that all the years I had assured myself that I was doing myself no physical harm with my behaviour, I was dangerously mistaken.

I had been diagnosed with hepatitis C while I was in the programme at the Ley. I seemed to manage this without any problems, which was just as well, as I wasn't ever offered any treatment. I didn't worry about it very much. Years after graduating from the Ley, I developed diabetes. I thought that I was managing this quite well until I was told that my diabetes was out of control and that I now had insulin-dependent diabetes. This was a real shock, and something I found really difficult to come to terms with. For a start, it meant that I had to inject myself several times each day in order to stay alive. This took me back to my junkie days. When I had first started at the Ley, I had promised myself that I would never inject again. Yet here I was, having to do it to survive.

I think it took me about a year before I really started to accept this was something I had to deal with for the rest of my life. I also realised that alcohol played a role with both my diabetes and hepatitis. I drank regularly and really enjoyed a few pints in the local pub with my mates. This was having a big impact on my illnesses. I had already given up drugs and even packed up smoking and now I decided that I had to give up drinking. This was a huge deal for me, as I cherished the release of going down the pub, and socialising enabled me to cope with the pressures of my emotionally demanding job.

I decided it would be a good idea to go on holiday with my mates for a last blow-out before giving up drinking for good. We went to Spain and spent the whole week reliving our youth and generally drinking as much as we could. How I didn't kill myself I do not know. When I look back on this time I can't believe I behaved so irresponsibly. Someone must have been looking after me. I had my last pint ever in Spain, approximately thirteen years ago. My life changed.

I found the transition from drinker to non-drinker really difficult. Mates would keep asking me to have a drink in my local pub. They said that I was a miserable bastard without a pint. "One drink won't kill you Steve," they said. I thought differently. It was a very difficult time for me, and I tried to fill my extra time constructively. I was still doing my motocross, and spent a bit more time in my garage working on my bikes. About a year after giving up drinking, I treated myself to a brand-new 1200 Harley Davidson Street Rod. I still have my Harley to this day and have the pleasure of riding it when the weather is good. I have ridden as far as southern Spain on my Harley, and find nothing more exhilarating than the sense of freedom that it gives me.

Not long after the trip to Spain, I was getting ready to go to a motocross meeting when I started to feel quite ill. I was coughing up loads of blood, so I went straight to the doctor. He told me to go home, pack a bag and make my way to Banbury Cottage Hospital, where I was expected. Once I got to the hospital, I was examined and told not to drink or eat anything as they were going to do exploratory investigations to find out what the problem was.

Following the examination, I was told that I was in a serious condition because I had burst varices. I had no idea what this meant. Apart from feeling a bit weak, I didn't think there was much wrong and wanted to know when I could go home because I didn't like being away from my family and from work. It was only after spending a week in hospital that I realised the significance of the situation. I could have died. The doctors warned me that the problem could recur at any time. I had three varices in my oesophagus and one in my stomach. Once I started to realise the full implications of this, I became quite frightened. Not long after being discharged from hospital, I returned to work. I had been told by the doctor that I had to be very conscious of my blood pressure. This was obviously difficult, working in the stressful environment of the Ley, so I just carried on as usual.

In 2008 came the big one. I was under Dr Ellis at Banbury. I had been seeing him for a number of years because of my varices. I had some ultrasound tests done, and following this I had to have a CT scan. I was asked to attend Dr Ellis's surgery on the evening of the 20th January 2008. I was very concerned; the appointment was in the evening, which made me quite suspicious. Friends around me tried to convince me that there was nothing sinister for me to worry about. I duly arrived for the appointment, and was asked into Dr Ellis's consulting room. Dr Ellis could see that I was quite anxious and started talking to me in a very matter-of-fact way about the issues that I had been seeing him for over the past few years.

"There is a way to cure a lot of your problems, Steve," he said. "You could have a new liver." I did not have a clue what he was talking about and just sat there and laughed.

"I don't understand what you are talking about – just tell me straight," I said.

Dr Ellis told me that I had a lesion on my liver. I still did not know what he meant.

He gave it to me straight. "Look, Steve," he said. "You have liver cancer."

I was completely shot away by this piece of news. After all I had gone through in my life, I did not want to be beaten by liver cancer. I was given two options: have a transplant, or die. Neither seemed very attractive at the time. The odds on the transplant being a success were not great.

"Will you think about having a transplant, Steve?" Dr Ellis asked me. At that moment in time I wasn't sure. I had thought that I had come to terms with my past, but I did wonder if I was good enough to have a transplant. What made *me* deserve a second chance, after all the terrible, awful things I had done in my life? While some people develop liver cancer through no fault of their own, I had brought it upon myself by consuming substances that are known to be extremely damaging to health. It was all my own fault.

Even later when I was told that I had been assessed, and was a suitable candidate for a transplant, I kept wondering if I really deserved to live. Should I have a year or so living my life to the full, spending time with my son, or should I take the biggest risk of my life and have a transplant knowing that there was a chance that I would die on the operating table? Should I take the liver when someone else, who deserved it more, had to continue to wait?

I needed time to think. After leaving the hospital that evening, I went over to see Bev and Norm, good friends of mine, to break the news. They were as shocked as I was, but offered me and my family support. Dr Ellis gave me two weeks to make up my mind. Time was not on my side. My lesion was 2.3 centimetres, and if it grew to 3 centimetres it would be too late to have a transplant, as it would be too big.

I spent the next two weeks considering my options. It was a nightmare. I didn't have a family – in the traditional sense – to consult with; my family was the community and the people I worked with, my wife and a few close friends. I did not keep the cancer a secret, as I felt that it was only right to make people aware of what was going on for me. I continued to work full-time and was supported by those around me.

At one stage, I decided that I definitely would not go ahead with the operation. Because of my past, I had convinced myself that the transplant would not be successful as I was not worthy of receiving some-body else's liver. What right did I have as a recov-ered addict to benefit from the death of an innocent human being? This was hard stuff to deal with. At other times, I felt that I had to go through with the transplant so that I didn't desert my son, as I had deserted my other children. I wanted to be there for him and help guide him as he grew up.

I don't think I actually came to a complete deci-sion at all. I returned to Dr Ellis for my appoint-ment after two weeks. I told him about my fears and anxieties. I had been seeing him for many years and he knew me well. He convinced me that we should move forward and have an assessment to find out my suitability for a transplant. Dr Ellis suggested I go to either Birmingham or Cambridge for the opera-tion. A good friend at the Ley has a brother who is a surgeon, and she told me that the best place in the world for a liver transplant was King's College Hospital in London. I asked Dr Ellis if I could be seen there. He was delighted to offer this to me, as that was where he had done his training and he knew all the surgeons who would deal with me. I felt I was going full circle – back to London, not ten miles from where I was born.

I continued to go to work every day and waited to hear from the hospital. A date was set for the assessment. I spent a week at King's, undergoing masses of tests. When it came to it, I was desperate to be found suitable for a transplant. At least then I would have a choice. At King's I was in the same ward as those who had undergone transplants already. I spent some time talking with them, which gave me some confidence for the procedure ahead. I was successful in my assessment and would have to wait until I was put on the transplant list.

On 18th June 2008, I was formally put on the liver transplant list. This meant I had to have my mobile phone on day and night and take it with me always. I could receive a call at any time. I was not allowed to go far from home. I had to be able to get to King's via hospital transport within a couple of hours. I continued to work full-time, but my mind was racing. Every time my mobile went off or my phone rang at home, I thought, "That's it; I'm off."

At six in the evening on Wednesday the 16th July 2008, I received the call. I spoke to a transplant coordinator who informed me that there might be a suitable liver for me and to expect hospital transport in the next thirty minutes. I called my friends Bev, Norm, Chris and Sue. Chris and Sue came over to look after Daniel, and Bev would come with me and Alison and provide support. All four friends arrived within twenty minutes, closely followed by an ambulance. I was in tears. I remember saying goodbye to Daniel, not knowing whether I would see him again. My friends were emotional too, but they tried to put on a brave face for me. Alison, Bev and I got into the ambulance and we were on our way.

"This is it," I thought. I was elated that a suitable liver had been found for me, but scared at the same time. I couldn't really get my head round it. As it happened, I didn't have to. We were on the M4 heading towards London when the ambulance driver received a call from King's. The liver was not suitable, and we had to turn back. This news was unbelievable. I didn't know whether to laugh or cry. After getting back home I sat down and relaxed. "Thank God for that," I thought. I had been saved for a while. I returned to work the next day, and everything went back to normal.

On Wednesday 23rd July, I received a phone call at quarter past eight in the evening. It was the liver transplant co-ordinator from King's. It was on again. My friends came round again and Alison, Bev and I headed to London. I was a bit more relaxed this time, partly because I expected to be called back to Oxford as we were driving along. This did not happen. We arrived at King's and I was wheeled into the ward.

"This is *really* it," I thought. I was scared now. There was no going back. The doctor came to take my blood, which was a performance in itself. As an ex-addict. I knew that I had only one good vein. I told the doctor this, told him where it was, and said that it would be difficult to obtain blood from me. They knew best. After about twenty puncture holes, the doctor passed me over to a competent nurse who listened to what I was saying and got blood straight away. I was a bit stressed out at this stage but I bore the doctor no ill will.

I was asked to shower in readiness for the operation. I did this and got into bed. I waited. And waited. At about half past four in the morning, the liver transplant coordinator came to see me. She apologised and said that unfortunately the liver was not suitable. I was gutted. Would a suitable liver *ever* be found for me?

We all returned home by train. Everything seemed too surreal to be believed. I returned to work the next day and everything went back to normal. On 20th August at eight in the morning, I received another call. It was the liver transplant coordinator. I should expect an ambulance in the next thirty minutes. From the coordinator's tone of voice, I could tell this was different.

Daniel was dropped off at the child-minder's, and Bev made her way to my house. On this occasion, an ambulance estate car pulled up and we climbed in. The blue flashing lights were on, and so was the siren. The driver meant business.

I remember that the cars on the motorway did not seem to move over for us very quickly, but as soon as we got to London it was like the parting of the seas; it was magic. At one point we went round a roundabout the wrong way. As we got nearer and nearer to King's, I expected to get a call saying that the liver was not suitable.

We arrived at King's within the hour and went straight to the ward, where I was booked in. Loads of people were looking after me. Grace, the transplant coordinator, introduced herself to me and told me that I would be receiving a split liver. Part of the liver had been removed and, as we spoke, was being given to a tiny baby. I would receive the larger part. I was told that the surgeons doing the operation for the baby would then do my operation. In one way, I was pleased, because it meant that the liver was of excellent quality. But, on the other hand, it meant that the healing process would be more difficult.

Before the operation, some blood had to be taken from me. An anaesthetist tried and, after a few attempts and many apologies, managed to get just enough for tests to be run. She then had to get a line in my foot for further blood. I was asked to shower with a special shower wash. I insisted on doing this on my own. When I returned from the shower, I sat down in a chair. Grace sat down at my level and looked me straight in the eyes.

"You do realise, Steve," she said, "that you will be getting your new liver today. The operation is definitely going ahead."

A couple of tears rolled down my face but I didn't say anything. I was in shock.

"Fuck it," I thought. "I'm here now, and they are the experts. I'm in their hands."

Thirty minutes later, I was being wheeled out of the ward. It was quite comical for all of us to be in the lift together as my wife and friends accompanied me upstairs. We only just fitted in! I was wheeled through double doors into a small holding area.

It was time to say goodbye before they took me into theatre. Alison kissed me and Bev gave me a hug. I didn't say anything. As they left, the doors in front of me opened and I saw the operating theatre and the surgeons. There were lights everywhere and everything seemed to happen so quickly. I was out of the game in seconds, and in the hands of the very gifted surgeons at King's.

The operation started at half past one in the afternoon. By four, my old liver had been taken out. This left me in a very precarious position. My old liver could not be put back in again, and my new liver was not yet connected. I couldn't function without a liver. Alison and Bev waited in the family room. It became apparent that the operation was going to take a bit longer than they thought. Finally, Alison and

Bev decided to check into a hotel. I had insisted that I wanted Alison to be there when I came round, but nobody knew when that would happen. Alison had told the staff that she could be contacted by phone at any time, and that both she and Bev would come to King's when I came round.

At nine o'clock that night, Grace called Alison to tell her that the operation was complete and that I was stable. Alison and Bev both visited me once I had been cleaned up – though of course I have no recollection of this, as I was sedated. They were also due to come and see me at seven thirty the next morning when I would be coming round. Instead, Alison received a call saying that I was to be kept on the ventilator and they would call her later.

They tried again to bring me round at about two o'clock on the afternoon of the 21st, but I was having none of it. At half past five they told Alison that it was unlikely I would come round that day. This was very upsetting for them. Alison and Bev were told that I would be brought round the next morning, so they arrived at about half past eight. They waited and waited.

Eventually, they were allowed into the intensive care unit, where I was in and out of consciousness and not in my right mind. Waking up was terrifying. I felt that I was engaged in an enormous battle with someone or something. Knowing me, my adversary was probably myself. The nurse had instructed Alison and Bev to talk to me, as it was probable that I could hear and understand what they were saying. Bev recalls that at one stage she stood at the end of the bed and looked me in the eye.

"You are in King's College Hospital, Steve," she said. "You have just had your liver transplant."

"I know where I fucking am," I said, looking straight at her. "Stop saying that." This produced fits of laughter from Alison and Bev and from Ferdinand, the nurse. I remember being very agitated as I was coming round, and that I kept shouting, "Hold on, hold on. Please!" It was as though I was fighting for my life. I recall pictures flashing through my mind. All I could see were black demons chasing me, and gargoyles trying to eat me. I had to put up the fight of my life. It was so very real and frightening. I was back in a black hole, desperately trying to fight my way out.

As I came round, the demons began to fade away, and I felt I was winning the battle. I was still questioning whether I was worthy of saving, whether I deserved the opportunity of a new liver. This really troubled me, especially given my past. I was becoming more lucid and coherent by the minute. I was swaddled in bandages and felt like a baby. I wanted to get free. At one point, I remember thinking that if I asked Bev nicely she might help me. When Alison was talking to Ferdinand, I called Bev over quietly.

"Sshh," I whispered. "Please help me out and take the bandages off my hands."

Bev looked at me. "I can't do that," she said. She knew that I had previously tried to pull all the leads out of my body.

"Well, fuck off then," I said. Bev just laughed. Everyone kept telling me I was doing OK, but it didn't feel like it. I felt helpless and unable to do anything for myself. This caused me great distress. Before I was allowed out of intensive care, the surgeon came in and asked me some questions, to find out whether I was compos mentis or not. He asked me my name, my age and my address, where I was and whether I knew what had happened. I remember thinking that I could have a laugh with him and say something silly, but I didn't. When he asked me who the prime minister was I told him I didn't have a fucking clue! I was deemed fit enough to go onto the main ward.

I can remember lying on my bed, brushing what I thought was sand off my chest. I asked Alison if she could see the sand. To my surprise, she said that she could not, but to me it remained very real. I was still hallucinating. On another occasion, I had a particularly bad night. I was shaking all over, and thought that I had actually started to burn my new liver out. I called the nurse and told her. She reassured me that this was not the case and said that I should try to relax.

I remained in King's for six weeks, and was then allowed to go home. I was tremendously pleased to be going home, but I was terribly frail and had lost a great deal of weight. I had aged ten years and looked a shadow of my former self.

I had worked right up until the day of my transplant, and it was very important to me that I visit the community to speak to residents and reassure them that I was OK. Rightly or wrongly, I am seen as the figurehead of the Ley. I had received letters and cards from residents throughout my time at King's. They had given me the strength to carry on.

I made the decision to visit work about eight weeks after my transplant. I was still unable to drive, and a friend picked me up to bring me to work. A new chief executive had arrived in my absence, and I wanted to check out how things were going, and to reassure myself and the residents that all was well. The stability of the community is always at the forefront of my mind, and a liver transplant didn't change that.

I arrived at about ten in the morning and asked for all residents and staff to join me. It was obvious from the look on some of the staff members' and residents' faces that they were shocked by my physical appearance. I stood in front of them all, thanked them for their kind support and told them how important it was to me. I explained that I hoped to be back at work very soon. The encounter was very emotional for us all. They were not used to seeing me like this, but I was determined to return when I was physically strong. I returned to work part-time three months after my liver transplant.

Words cannot express how grateful I am to the surgeons and all the other staff at King's who helped me through my operation and subsequent recovery.

A day doesn't go past without me thinking that somebody somewhere lost someone they loved, and I cannot thank them enough for allowing their liver to be given to me, to give me new life. I am truly grateful to them.

Because of all the drama surrounding the transplant, I lost sight for a little while of how difficult this period was for Daniel, who was still very young. I was too busy fighting to keep myself alive to notice or think about the trauma that he was going through. I regret not having thought about this before the operation, as I might have been able to do something to prepare him for how difficult it was going to be. Shortly after the procedure, all Daniel was able to say was that he didn't want to talk about it. It was only after a year or two that he started talking about the operation and its aftermath. I know that he still worries about me because he understands that I have health issues and am more likely to get sick than other people because I am on immune suppressants every day. I do my best to reassure him without sugar-coating the truth.

At the time of writing, Daniel is just approaching adolescence. He is the only one of my children I've always been there for; the first time I didn't negate my responsibilities. I am pleased to say that my step-daughter and daughter, who still live in Cardiff, are in regular contact with me and pleased with how I have been able to change from the chaotic man they used to know. Sadly, their mother, Anne, died about five years ago. She had never managed to win her battle with addiction, and one day she fell and slipped into a coma. Nobody knows what drugs she had been taking. She never woke up.

Perhaps Michelle and Catherine and I are not as close as some families, but I hope that they know that I will always be there for them when they need me, and I am sure that they would do the same for me. They are still very good sisters and very supportive of each other. Michelle has made me a grandfather. Catherine is a lesbian, and for a long time I was concerned that this was not her own choice or inclination, but that I had literally turned her off men because I had been such an awful father. It was a difficult subject to broach, but eventually I managed to ask her about it, and she laughed and reassured me that that wasn't the case; that she had been born gay and was very happy that way.

Although I've had a very chequered past, I think that I have done useful work at the Ley, and I am proud of it. While I have no problems with daily reading and writing, I am not what you would call a literary man. I write letters, but I leave the lengthy reports to others. I think that my strength lies in the fact that I know what our recovering addicts are going through, because I have been there too, and I have come out the other side.

I expect to spend the rest of my life – whatever time I have left – working in the field of drug rehabilitation, right here at the Ley Community. Anyone who works in this field knows that it's a job that calls for immense dedication. It's about working alongside people you genuinely care about, and giving them the best when they need it, whatever day of the week that happens to be. I plan to stay here for as long as I can be of help.

I still love motorbikes and cars, and a beautiful vehicle makes my heart race just as it did when I was in the workshop with my uncle Albie. As well as my health problems and my love of bikes, there are many other reminders of the man I used to be; the tough guy I thought I was. I still have my tattoos. I thought they made me look so tough when I was kid, but on a man of my age, they look quite different. I have considered having them removed, but then I thought, "No; they are part of who I am."

The Ley offered me the chance to start my life again. The first day I really began to realise this was the one when I was given the little elephant, with a white patch and red stitches, to remind me always of a very special time in my life. I still have my elephant to this day. It is very significant to me, and I will treasure it always.

There was a period in my life when I was concerned about what people thought of me. I worried that I would be judged on my past and considered a bad person. But I'm not a bad person, and I think that everyone who knows me can see that I am not the man I used to be and never will be. I am not perfect but I do genuinely care about people and I like to help people make changes. I never stop being grateful to the Ley for everything that it has done for me and I hope that I will always be able to do my best for it and for the people in our programme.

Over the course of the years that I've been here, the programme at the Ley has evolved, developed and grown. We now have a range of buildings, and rooms for sixty-four residents. It has been exciting to be here throughout all the developments we have seen. We continue to help addicts from all different walks of life. Many of our graduates have been successful. Of course, there have also been disappointments, when former residents returned to drug-taking, or ended in prison, or even dead. But most of our graduates have succeeded in their recovery, and many of them have ended up doing very well. They include social workers, probation officers, academics, housewives, gardeners, wealthy business people, mechanics… really every sort of person imaginable. Many have gone on to become mothers and fathers, or have been able to rekindle family relationships that had been damaged by their destructive behaviour and drug-taking. We stay in touch with a lot of them and are always happy to hear from them, or from their families. We know that the work we do has made an inestimable difference to so many lives. I think that I probably know that better than most people.

I am proud that the Ley won a prestigious Centre for Social Justice Award in 2010 for its effectiveness, efficiency, innovation and compassion, and that we continue to hold a three-star excellence rating with our regulators, the Care Quality Commission. In 2011, I won an Oxfordshire High Sheriff Award, and I was also invited to the Queen's Garden Party. The Ley continues to move onward and upward.

I sometimes think about the friends I lost along the way, throughout my years of resentment and chaos. Would they want to meet me now? Would they still be angry with me for all the betrayals, or happy that I have been able to sort things out? Since my dear friend Brian and I parted ways, for example, our journeys must have been completely different. Perhaps some of my old friends will read this book; maybe we'll even meet. If that does happen, I'll have to take it as it comes. I am not the same person I was when they knew me, but nor am I someone completely different.

At the time of writing, I have been working at the Ley Community for half my life. I spent the first half of my life fucking things up for myself and I hope that I have spent the subsequent years not just making things better for me and those I love, but also helping people who are in the situation that I was in years before. I hope that, in at least some ways, the Ley and all the work that we have done together have made it possible for me to become the man I was always supposed to be.

Epilogue

You will be aware from reading my book that obstacles have presented themselves to me on numerous occasions in my life. I did think, rather foolishly, that my life had settled down. As it turns out, this is not the case.

I had been having regular check ups at King's Hospital in London and had no reason to think that there were any problems. In December 2011 I went to London again and saw my consultant. I assumed this would be a straightforward check up and had no need to be alarmed. However, I noticed straight away that the doctor's manner was very different to the previous occasions I had seen him. I noticed that he was more serious and I could tell from his body language that all was not well. I was instantly on high alert. He informed me that my Hepatitis C condition had returned and had escalated enough for him to advise me to have treatment. I knew when I had my transplant that although my liver would be brand new, the Hep C within my body may eventually attack the liver, but I did not realise how quickly this might happen. Since I'd had Hep C twenty years previous to my transplant I wasn't sure what this would actually mean. The doctor told me that things were different this time, I had a new liver and I was on Tacrolimus (an anti-rejection drug) as well as many other drugs to keep me alive. I am also chronically diabetic. Because of all this I was told that the Hep C was life-threatening for me. I asked many questions about treatment, prognosis etc. and wondered whether I would have enough fight in me again to see this one through. I was given choices. I could do nothing and eventually the sclerosis in my liver (caused by the Hep C) would return requiring me to have another liver transplant. I knew that I could never go through that again so I discounted this option straight away. The wait, the uncertainty of finding a suitable liver together with the trauma and repercussions for my family just made it unthinkable to go down that route. I consider myself to be a bit like a cat with nine lives, though I feel I have lived 11 lives already. I'm not sure I would be so lucky again.

I could have treatment but was told that I would have to start this sooner rather than later as, having had a transplant, the Hep C would be very virulent.

My immediate feelings were of fear. I had known many other people who had undergone treatment only to suffer serious side effects and eventually stop the treatment. This would not be an option for me – if I stopped the treatment it would eventually kill me. However I had witnessed friends at first hand who had undergone treatment and suffered very badly psychologically, physically and mentally. This had been so extreme that I knew of people who had tried to commit suicide. This was extremely disturbing for me. If you recall earlier in my book I described how difficult it was for me to come round after my liver transplant and the doctors said that this was probably due to the effects of illicit drugs in my body all those years ago. I have also mentioned my psychiatric past, so you'll know that anything that might be potentially mind-altering is a very frightening prospect for me. And, not just for me, but for those around me, particularly my teenage son who was going through his own life changes which I was already finding difficult to manage. This seemed like a recipe for disaster. But what choice did I have? If I did nothing my son wouldn't have a father. Here I was again. I could be deserting the only child I have ever been a proper father to, albeit through no fault of my own. I had promised myself I would get it right this time. I can't help thinking that this may not be the case if things don't work out – if I cannot deal with the treatment psychologically I know I can never have another full liver transplant. I just wouldn't be able to do it.

My consultant thought I would be suitable to go on a treatment trial that was an alternative to Interferon, which I didn't particularly want to take.

He called me to discuss this. I was told that if the trial proved to be successful my long term prospects would be significantly better. I was slightly reassured by this and wanted to give it a go. I informed the consultant that I would prefer to start sooner rather than later, in the summer months, as I felt this would be better for me emotionally. He said he would get onto it. I left Kings feeling quite positive and received a letter shortly afterwards confirming all that I had been told.

My next appointment at Kings was in March. I felt quite buoyant and thought I would be given a start date. I was wrong. I saw a different consultant this time and was informed that there were no trials available for the next four years, that he didn't know anything about the offer that had been made to me previously and there was no record of any letter having been sent out to me. I was gutted; I was expecting to start treatment and wanted to get on with it. I had been very anxious about the future, accepted that I needed to do it and felt that all the hopes I had had been dashed. I was back to square one, very familiar territory for me. The consultant asked me to provide him with a copy of the letter that I had been sent regarding the trial. I was appalled that this had not been recorded on my file. I questioned whether the experts were taking my life seriously. Was I sitting on a time bomb or not? I drove home to Oxford feeling as though my last few meetings at Kings had been a complete waste of time. I located the letter and faxed it through to the consultant. He acknowledged this and, as well as telling me he was in America for a week, he said that because of the drugs I have to take I may not actually be suitable for the trial after all. Brilliant – six months has passed and I am no further forward. My fears and anxieties are heightened, and I don't know how much further the Hep C has progressed.

I have since been told that there is a possibility of me receiving treatment in Oxford which, to be honest with you, sounds like a much better proposition. Being on my doorstep it would mean I wouldn't have to travel to London regularly. However, until this has been verified I will not be referred onto Oxford. I wonder how long this will take? Not that I am looking forward to it, I have been told that I will have to have lots of tests done and be monitored very closely in order that my new liver does not get rejected. I will have to have an injection each week. This injection will physically and emotionally drain me to such an extent that I will not be able to do anything except rest all weekend. I worry about this a great deal. I have already explained to you how important my work at the Ley Community is and to contemplate not being able to function properly at work as I have done since three months after my liver transplant, makes me very anxious and fearful. If all this isn't enough, I also have the worry of the cocktail of drugs that I will be taking which may cause my liver to reject and could obviously be potentially life-threatening. It doesn't look good does it?

But, I'm a fighter. I don't lie down easily and certainly don't give in once I've got the bit between my teeth. I have so many things to fight for: my children, my job, the Ley Community, my family and my friends. There are so many things I still want to do: I have my passion for riding and would very much love to do another Harley Davidson Rally abroad and ride in the sunshine. Maybe I will even get to ride part of Route 66. Everyone has to have dreams and it's these thoughts that will help me fight the fight. I've thought it through and I recognise that I will need my family and friends to support me through this difficult time. One thing I do have is good friends. I very rarely ask much of my friends but I do know that that they are there for me.

There are some of you out there who will be thinking 'what goes around, comes around' and by that I mean that you think I am only getting what I deserve. I abused my body with illegal drugs and alcohol for many, many years and this is the price I pay for that. I don't disagree with you. But I've paid my dues, I've given back to society.

One thing I would like to say is that I am very grateful to all the people who have supported me, especially at Kings – the doctors and nurses who have managed to get me even as fit as I am today. It might sound as though I am ungrateful but this could not be further from the truth. I just want to live a bit longer. I'm sure you can understand that.

Acknowledgements

It would be quite impossible to list all the people who have helped me to write *Steve: Unwanted*. However, I feel I must mention Dr Alex Callum, who was instrumental in affording me the opportunity to turn my life around, and Dr Bertram Mandelbrote for allowing me entrance into the Ley Community. Ultimately, these two men saved my life.

I would like to take this opportunity to thank the Ley Community in assisting me with my recovery. Many people have touched my life; those residents and staff who were on the programme when I went through it and those who have been through the programme since I became a staff member. They are all very special people and have made me the man I am today.

It goes without saying that I could not have written this book without Bev Smith and Wendy Dawson. I thank them for all their hard work and patience in helping me, keeping me on track and generally keeping me in order!

A word on the author

I thought I'd seen everything, until my close friend Chris Lambrianou said to me one day, "Tel, I want to take you somewhere." After a short drive through leafy Oxford, we arrived at the Ley Community – a rehabilitation centre. I had never seen one before, but I'd always imagined they'd be like prisons – dirty and smelly, with the odd nutter talking to himself in the corner. I hadn't expected a lovely, tranquil, spotless "mini village"; people walking around, talking and laughing, against a backdrop that could have been a Constable painting.

Then Chris introduced me to a man called Steve Walker. Steve has an extremely warm character that he combines with a strong sense of purpose; this is a man whose work is his life. In fact, for Steve, his work is *other people's* lives. I wouldn't even try to guess how many people this special man has saved, giving them back their lives that had been stolen by addiction.

Steve Walker is a *real* hero. He's humane, kind, and he shows real affection to those who may never have experienced it before. The world needs men like Steve. He opened my eyes to many things, and I cherish many a lesson I've learned from him. And remember, when I went there, I thought I'd seen everything.

With huge affection to Steve, Chris and each and every warrior at the Ley Community.

Tel Currie, author and boxing promoter

What can I say about my friend? You haven't met him yet, but you will get to know him as you walk through the pages of his life. You will find every kind of emotion in Steve, except self-pity. If I were in the trenches, I would want him with me. Having shared many experiences with him over the years, I can only say he is a top bloke. And I am not alone when I say this. Ask the many people, young and old, whose lives he has saved. I have never known him to give up on anyone, even if they have given up on themselves. He has taken "lifers" out of prison and touched them when prison has failed to do so. He has taken young men and women off the streets and helped them to change their wretched lives, turning defeat into victory. How do I know? Well, for many years it was my job to bring these people to him.

Chris Lambrianou, author of *Escape from the Kray Madness, Do the Walls Come Down: Reflection of a Lifer*, winner of the Koestler Award for literature

Steve Walker's remarkable story – now movingly narrated in his first book – is inspirational. His journey offers a powerful example of how thousands of people can and do transform their lives, and become agents for change in others. Indeed, his story is a testament to why programmes like the Ley Community are essential resources in a state-of-the-art health system. Such communities transmit the fundamental message of recovery: *You alone can do it, but you can't do it alone.*

George De Leon – author of
The Therapeutic Community

Steve Walker is extraordinary. He's tough as old boots, but as emotionally open and vulnerable as anybody you're likely to meet. He lives and breathes the story of the Ley Community but he also understands change, and is big enough to make tough decisions. He is passionate and makes enemies along the way – especially when he shouts a lot – but he has attracted a massive following of people whose lives have been fundamentally touched by his example, his insight, his brutal honesty and his sheer determination to save others.

Jeremy Spafford

I was privileged to meet Steve Walker in Holland, and subsequently on a visit to the Ley Community in June 2009. He impressed me as a very mature person, who has been able to make use of, and reflect on, his own considerable life experience. Better still, he is able to use this in an objective way in his work. He had obviously earned the considerable respect of both staff and residents for his huge contribution to the growth and development of the Ley Community today. The Ley Community to me is the best of the current models in the UK of how a "Concept" Therapeutic Community should be, and Steve is an embodiment of all that this means.

David Warren-Holland

STEVE: INTERVIEWED

At what point in your life did it occur to you that there was enough in your past to fill a book? And what in particular did you want to achieve by writing it?

I've felt for some time now, I'd probably say over the last 15 years, that I could probably write a book. A number of people who have suggested the idea to me – for a number of reasons. One is a therapeutic reason for myself, to actually... unload, I suppose, my life, my lifestyle, and not to have something that for many, many years I've been ashamed of. Just clear the sheet and make myself feel a little bit better about myself.

My friend, Chris Lambrianou [an associate of the Krays, who served 15 years in prison for the murder of Jack "The Hat" McVittie], who writes books himself, was the man who really convinced me that it would be good for me to actually get it out, get it on paper, and give people the opportunity to see that people can reform and can change their life. And that's what I have done. I've relieved myself of all the things that I feel bad about. It's a kind of exorcism. I'm not suggesting for one minute that you can actually wipe that slate clean. I think you have to live with who you've been. But the reality is that I can move on, and I have moved on from that person, and I've done a lot of good for a lot of people since then.

How did you go about writing the book?

Well, it wasn't that difficult, because in my day to day work, here at the Ley Community, it's all about honesty, it's all about talking about your past, it's all about the here and now; what's been in the past and put behind you, put to rest. And so it wasn't difficult for me to bring up my life story and put it on paper. I've spent a lot of time working along with the residents within the community, and a lot of it's based on honesty, respect and trust. And you have to use the tools and the elements that you have in your life to try and help other people move through this kind of situation. So, for me, it was always there.

I think the difficult part was a long, long time ago – when I actually did the programme. And that was about being honest with myself. I think once I learned to be honest with myself, and not feel ashamed of where I'd been and what I'd done, then I realised I could use my past as a good tool to work with the residents in the programme. So to actually put it on paper... it's always there, it's always been fresh. I've never, I don't think, been able to forget about where I came from.

So how candid were you in the book? Is there anything you've left out, or have you put everything in it?

I don't think I've put everything in it. I think there are little bits and pieces that I could have been a bit more explicit about. And I think there are some things that perhaps I could have gone deeper into, but I don't think it would be beneficial to me or beneficial to anybody else... I suppose, in reality, there are many other things that I could probably talk about at some stage; I'm sure there are things I could elaborate on about my bad side. I haven't totally put everything down, but all the important stuff is there.

And are you pleased with the finished product?

Yes, I am. I'm very pleased. I'm not a big reader myself – and when I *do* read, I have to read a book that constantly flows. I'm a bit of a lazy reader. I'm dyslexic, and so therefore it has to be a bit riveting for me to keep involved, and I'm hoping that's what I've written.

How old were you when you learned to read?

I learned to read when I was 17, when I was in a detention centre. I was put into a cell on my own, and I couldn't read, and the only thing that was in there was the Bible. And there was I, locked up around 23 hours a day, with no one to talk to. And I decided that, even though it wasn't really what I wanted to look at, I should try and spend some of my time a bit more valuably…

Did you find the Bible a helpful book to have with you at that point?

Well, it certainly occupied my time. I'm not necessarily a religious person, but I do believe that there is a power greater than myself – whatever shape or form that is, I have no idea, but I do have some belief that there is always someone guiding me. I think in some respects I've been guided – I don't know whether it's by God, or who it's by. But I've had a bit of a guardian angel, I've had someone look after me, I've had someone help me to achieve what I've achieved in my life. But I don't know, I have no idea… the whole idea of me learning to read … I mean, I used to have to get other people to write my letters for me; I couldn't write letters home. It was a very, very bad kind of communication. In some ways it felt like someone had cut your tongue, like you couldn't respond to people outside, because the only way of communicating was by mail. So the Bible was useful to me because it helped me lift myself out of that.

Which parts of the book were the hardest to write?

The hardest parts to write were the things that I'm not so proud of. I worry about how people might perceive those things. And I worry about how people will look at me. And I worry whether this still matters to some people out there, whether there's still any rivalry about some of this stuff. I've been out of this situation for many, many years now, but some people have memories, and you don't know what sort of ghosts you're going to bring up... I've found some of that quite worrying. But there was no point in me writing the book unless I was going to be honest. Because the only way that I'm going to be able to help anybody to recognise that change is possible is by actually being honest. So there was reservation about it, but there was also part of me saying, well, you gotta go for it.

But it was difficult. And even ... you saying to me, are there any parts that I've left out. Well, yes, there are. Because you obviously have to think about some of the things that you've done and you think, well, you know, is that going to do me any good, and is that going to do anyone else any good? So you had to think about it. But all in all, a lot of it came as a flow, because it's a memory that I carry with me all the time. And there were some parts, as I was digging, that I felt uneasy about. But you work through it.

One of the things that comes across quite strongly in the book is that there's a big gap between Steve Walker 30 years ago, and Steve Walker now. But you're still the same man, you're still the same body and soul. What parts of yourself, today, do you think you share with your old self?

Well, that's a very good question… I think there's a part of me that still shares a lot of my old self. I just don't act the same. I can still think the same – I can still be the same person. But I've been given a choice, something that I didn't feel I had all those years ago. I was doing what I was doing because that's where I got involved, that became part of my life, that was part of my living, part of my existence, it was part of me *being* somebody. And so, all of those things that I used to do all those years ago, to be who I was then, I've actually just turned those things around. So it's the same kind of energy, but instead of me being so negative about life, being a person that took advantage of everything, and used everybody to my own needs, and being involved in all that violence… I use all my energies, and everything that I've experienced to different ends. I'm still a short-tempered kind of person, but it's for a different reason. It's not for my gain. It may be through frustration, you know, when you try to actually encourage people to make changes. It can become very frustrating when you feel like you're actually talking to yourself 30 years ago. So I still use the same kind of energies, but I've actually developed myself and I use the skills that I had and put them into a different perspective. I've gained a lot more knowledge and learned a lot more about myself.

Was there one particular moment when you made that switch, or was it more of a gradual process?

I think it's always been a gradual process, and I think you're always still learning – I'm still learning even today. But there was a point when I realised I no longer wanted to live a life, because I didn't like who I was, and I didn't like the way I was treating my family, my children, or anything else. I basically wanted out. I think the key to that was sitting in a hospital with my children's pictures on the wall, having no contact with them, no contact with anybody, thinking about what kind of bastard I'd been, thinking, "Do they deserve this?", and having people around me in that hospital who couldn't cater for themselves very well. And there I was, a fairly fit man, maybe not together in my head, but I had everything to go for, and there were people in there who were in terrible states. And there I was, throwing my life away, and these people were fighting for their lives. And I think the penny dropped, that I'd spent 15 years using drugs, I'd broken every rule, there wasn't anybody or anything that really mattered to me, apart from me having what I wanted, and all of a sudden what I'd wanted wasn't what I wanted any longer. And I didn't want to be that person any more.

So it was a conscious decision?

It was a very conscious decision, the changing, the making of the changes. By the time I came to the Ley Community, I'd made that decision. It wouldn't have mattered *what* they'd asked me to do. At that time, I could not stand the person I'd become, or who I was, any longer.

In the book you talk about one of the patients in the hospital who asked you to shave him, he couldn't even shave himself...

That's right. And that was so major for me. You know, he wanted to look smart for a visit, and there was me just carrying on taking all this stuff for granted, didn't give a damn about anyone or anything. And I thought, you know, "what is it with you? Get a grip. You've got all these things." And I think that was brought to me in some respects when it was me standing there, giving this guy a shave. I realised I could *do* something for somebody, that I'm not as useless as I actually thought I was.

Who, in your past, do you feel the most grateful to?

I think there are a few people that I'm very grateful to. In later life, I was more grateful to the people that tried to push me in the right direction, and one of those particular people was a guy called Dr Alex Callum, who always had a bit of faith in me, that I could make changes. He had more faith in me than I had in myself. And him encouraging me to come to rehab was one of the most important things. I also think that Dr Mandelbrote, the founder of the Ley Community, was another man who had faith in me when I didn't have any faith in myself, and gave me a chance. And the Ley Community, as well, I'm very, very grateful to, for the work and the time and the effort that they've put in.

As far as my family is concerned, I was very grateful to my grandparents for bringing me up. But I also went through a kind of mixed agenda with them. Because older people don't necessarily understand younger people. And there were certain things that I always remember being resentful about, about not being allowed to do what the other children were doing down the road, and stuff like that. I'm aware that they always tried to do their best for me. But it was very, very difficult for me, living in that kind of situation.

It seems quite crazy, really, that the people I feel most grateful to are people in authority, people that have given me a chance, when I didn't feel that I deserved a chance. It was a very strange thing for me. The next time that came up in my life was when I was going through the liver transplant. I constantly asked myself whether I was worthy of this chance, and it played on my mind quite a lot. Here I am, again, in a situation when I need something, and all I can think is, "Am I worthy?" Because I know who I've been, I know who I *am*. And I constantly questioned that.

I sort of thought that people who would be making decisions about whether I could actually have a transplant were people who weren't thinking about things from a medical point of view, but were thinking about judging me. Because I was sitting there in judgement of myself, and I was just thinking, "I wonder if these people think I'm worthy. I wonder if this is in the equation." And I really struggle with whether that should actually have happened for me. And I'm also very grateful to them. My transplant was nearly three years ago now, and as you can see I'm doing well, I'm doing OK. And that's the other thing about the guardian angel – I have no idea who it is, but I'm getting more than my fair share.

If your grandparents could see you now, do you think they'd be proud of you?

Yes, I do, yeah, I do think they'd be proud of me. They'd be proud of me and I think that they were always looking out for me. I'd never suggest that they were ever not doing their best for me. It's just that their way of doing it wasn't the way that I wanted it to happen for me. They travelled around the country to see me when I was in custody, or when I was in prison. They tried everything to help me, and I can always remember my grandmother saying, "It's not my Stevie, it's the people he hangs around with." And it's such a nice thought that she didn't feel it was down to me. But in actual fact, it *was* down to me, and what I became *was* me.

But do you think your grandmother's faith in you had an effect on how your life has transpired?

I can't say that there was a great deal of push from her or from my grandfather. I'd become so wayward that I'd left them behind, I'd left everything behind. By the time I got round to doing something about my life, I didn't really have many people left in my life, because I'd burned most of my bridges. So I can't say that they were very influential in that sense. But I always knew they wanted me to be a good boy they wanted me to get it right, and I know that their heart was in the right place. It's just that I couldn't deliver the goods.

And what about your father, would he be proud of you?

[Long pause] Funny relationship, my father, very funny relationship. I think in some ways he would be proud of what I've done, because as far as most people are concerned, I completely turned the odds around. I didn't speak to him for probably 25 years, right up until just before he was dying, when I wanted to make amends to our relationship, because I felt that, whatever had happened, my father ended up in the situation he was in – yes, it probably had some-thing to do with himself – but I also think that that was the way the cards were dealt for him, and that's the way that he lived. I don't think he was strong enough to make the changes I've made, and I can't

hold it against him. I genuinely believe that there have got to be some things that came up in his life that made it very, very difficult. I know that he was a very jealous man. I know that he was very possessive... very angry man... But I wanted, I actually wanted to make him aware that – no matter what'd gone on, he was still my father. And I wasn't going to go there and curse him, or whatever, I was going there to help him, so that when he did die, there was a chance that he could actually die with a bit of dignity and respect, instead of feeling bad about himself, like I knew I felt about myself. I'm sure he must have felt shit about himself and the life that he'd led, and how he'd responded to me, and those kinds of things. I just wanted to help him, maybe just say, "Well, OK, that's gone, we're not going to worry about that any more." And that's how he left this world. That's how it ended for him.

Did he seem grateful to you?

Yes, he did. Yes, he was very grateful to me, I know he was very grateful to me. I was the one who was running backwards and forwards to Kent to see him when he was in hospital, I took him home on one occasion... It was OK. And I had my few words with him after he'd died – went to see him in the chapel of rest. Just made it clear.

What was the appeal of the criminal lifestyle to you? How did it make you feel?

Well, I can honestly say that I don't think I went into the crime element because I wanted to. I think I went into the crime element because of the people I mixed with, because of the background I came from; not going to a very smart school, being dyslexic, feeling put down in the classroom, all this kind of stuff ... all led to the life of crime. And being put down, made to look like a dunce standing in the corner, having people laughing at me, finding it quite amusing that I was thick. And then having bullies around me, having things taken off me... I had to find a way to live, you know. And my way of living, unfortunately, went the way that it did. I got sick and tired of being bullied by the bully, so I became the bully. Then I found that being a bully actually felt quite good, because I was getting away with whatever I wanted to get away with. And if you take it further, obviously, as life went along, things escalated...

But I didn't feel that I belonged anywhere, and it was about feeling that I had somewhere where I belonged. I actually belonged with the criminal fraternity – people who were involved in doing these terrible things. It had some kind of excitement. And the whole idea of trying to fund some of the things I wanted to do through the back door became quite interesting to me. And as it went along, the more I got involved, the more I started to recognise how much I could actually *earn*, how well off I could be, the more

I continued down that particular path. So it's not something that I feel proud about, but it's something that happened. And I don't think I'm the only person that happens to – I think there are a lot of people that it happens to. And that's why it's so appropriate for me to write a book like this: so that other people who think, "I'm on that slope, I've been there, I've felt this," can be inspired to make a bit of a change.

Do you ever miss that side of you life?

I think I do miss it. Because there was a lot of excitement. And when you take something away from someone's life, you have to replace it with something. My replacement started with the Ley Community, my time here, bringing me back to some sort of normality, after spending 15 years wayward, you know, reminding me of some of the things that I love, some of the passion that I had. I wanted to make some changes so I went to work on lorries – when I first left the programme I became a lorry fitter, something I'd wanted to do for years. Being involved in muck and oil and grease was really important to me. It meant that I could *fix* something. It's important to me to be able to *fix* something. Working with the people at the Ley Community is about helping somebody to fix something. I was in the fixing business, I could fix particular things, I could do something.

Then there's the whole thing about excitement. When you're breaking the law and you're doing bad things, it's something about the excitement – being wanted, being chased, being a villain, or whatever. So I came back to my old love, riding motorbikes. The adrenalin I got from stealing and all that kind of stuff – I was getting my natural adrenalin back, without using drugs, without using anything else. It became natural. So I think that my replacement was all about bikes, and all about something I can be involved in.

There's a whole side of me that's still very passionate about speed, risk, and all of that… I mean, it explains brilliantly in some respects, what we were talking about a little bit earlier, that everything I do today – some of the stuff's still very risky. You know, I still race occasionally, got a nice fast car. So all my general needs are being met by an alternative mechanism. Whereas, before, it was being met by deceit, stealing, robbing, cheating. So it's the same excitement completely – in a different way.

Do you ever miss the drugs?

No. I don't take any drugs. I don't drink. I don't smoke. Over the thirty years I've worked here, and the things that I've gone through, I've no desire to get involved in any of that stuff.

What would have happened if you'd never ended up in the Ley Community?

I genuinely believe that if I hadn't come to the Ley Community I'd have been dead by now, there's no doubt about it. All the time, all the years that I'd been using, it didn't really matter to me whether I lived over 40, 50, 60 – it was never important to me. My life was on a knife edge, it always had been, and I was fully aware of that. And if I hadn't have come to the Ley, there's no doubt about it, I wouldn't be alive today. If I'd have continued doing what I was doing, nobody would have ever confronted me about my behaviour, how it affected others, and what I needed to do to make those changes without actually being put into rehab. And I genuinely believe that the Ley Community was the right one, even though I did not try any other. Because there was nothing more in your face than coming here and being asked those difficult questions: "Who the fuck do you think you are?" "What gives you the right to do these things to other people?" "You're a father. What sort of a father are you?" Those kinds of questions I needed to be put to me hard and fast, and I didn't need anybody holding back any punches, because I needed to find out what I was. And the only way I could find out what I was, was by people being upfront, honest and direct with me. And no matter how painful that was, that's what I needed, and I'm a strong believer in old traditions; I needed to be treated in the way that I was treating others to make me realise how it felt to be on the receiving end. And there weren't many places around that would have been able to do that to a person like myself. So, for me, the Ley was my saviour.

And was it a lucky break that you ended up here? Or do you think it was fated in some way, your guardian angel at work again?

Well, I did actually apply to come to the Ley about 18 months before that. I actually got somebody else to fill in the application forms for me. As I told you, I'm not very good at that sort of stuff. And all of a sudden a good bag of drugs came along, a good bit of gear, and I got deterred.

But I think fate plays a very good part in some stuff that happens to people, and... here I am!

What would you do if your son showed any interest in taking drugs?

I genuinely believe that I've always been very honest with him about what I do and where I work, what the dangers are and stuff like that. I'd like to think that some of the stuff that I've been teaching him perhaps wouldn't take him down that road. Nevertheless, if he did, I'd have to take into consideration how to go about that, and help him to perhaps discover a different way. My son does have dyslexia, my son is very dyslexic, and basically I do as much as I possibly can right now to help him do things that he feels good about – he's very good at sport, he's very good at karate, he rides motocross, he does lots and lots of different things. Those opportunities are available to him not because I'm spoiling him, but because I'm giving him an outlet where I didn't get an outlet. So I'd like to think that part of what I'm doing may be a deterrent from that situation.

He actually comes into work with me on occasions. He talks to the residents, he knows quite a lot about what goes on with drugs and alcohol. He got taken to the library at school last year, and the school was very alarmed because he started picking up books about drugs and addiction. They actually got in touch with us to say that they were quite concerned about what his choice of something to read was. And my wife said that the situation is that he knows what his dad does for a living, he knows what his dad's been up to, and he's just looking for some sort of understanding. I'd like to think that that's not going to happen, but then again, on the other hand, it may. Whatever happens, I don't think you can force anybody to make any choices. I will try and be as supportive as I possibly can, but I would be a hard taskmaster. I'd make some big hurdles and try and help him jump them.

If you could talk to yourself when you were your son's age, what advice would you give yourself?

[Long pause] I basically think the damage was already done for Steve Walker by 12. I think the damage was done a lot earlier for Steve. I think what I would like to say to him is, don't make the same mistakes as myself. I think that would be the strongest thing. I'm not suggesting that at that particular time I was all bad, because I wasn't. But I think my life make-up had already been put on me, and I was acting it. By that time I'd got into bullying at school,

rebelling... and I know this happens with everyone. But I mean to *strong* extremes; not just telling your mum and dad to piss off – really acting it out. I think the rot had already set, and I was going along these roads...

What would you like to be remembered for?

I think I'd like to be remembered as someone who has managed to turn their life around, and in doing so, has managed to help a lot of other people; have that kind of recognition, I suppose, that not all was bad. It may have started bad, but at the end of the day, the bad boy came good.

Steve Walker is now Programme Director of the Ley Community in Oxfordshire, one of Britain's most important and successful drug rehabilitation centres, where he was treated in the late 1980s and early 1990s.

OTHER TITLES FROM SHORT BOOKS:

Crimson China
Betsy Tobin

ISBN 9781907595226   Paperback £7.99

"Unforgettable" - Sue Gee
"Gripping" - *Financial Times*
"Unbearably tense" - *Guardian*

February 2004, Morecambe Bay.
Angie, an English woman haunted by her past.
Wen, a Chinese cockle picker fighting for a future.

One freezing night Angie wades into the sea in a drunken bid to commit suicide; instead she finds herself saving Wen's life.

They share neither language nor experience but Angie offers him sanctuary, soon finding in this enigmatic stranger a refuge of her own.

What she doesn't know is that Wen is a wanted man, on the run from a criminal gang who pose just as great a threat as the icy waters of Morecambe Bay...

"This fine novel grows in pace and power, propelled by a vividly drawn cast and a gradually building sense of jeopardy as the snakeheads close in" - *Daily Mail*

The House on Paradise Street
Sofka Zinovieff

ISBN 9781907595691   Paperback £7.99

"I can't remember when I was so totally absorbed by a book...
Enthralling, moving and wise."
Cressida Connolly

Athens, 1942:
Two sisters divided by politics and tragedy...

In 2008 Antigone Perifanis returns to her old family home in
Athens after 60 years in exile. She has come to attend the funeral of her only son, Nikitas, who was born in prison, and
whom she has not seen since she left him as a baby.

Nikitas had been distressed in the days before his death
and, curious to find out why, his English widow Maud starts
to investigate his complicated past. In so doing, she finds herself reigniting a bitter family feud, discovering a heartbreaking
story of a young mother caught up in the political tides of the
Greek Civil War and forced to make a terrible decision that
would blight not only her life but that of future generations...

The House on Paradise Street is an epic tale of love and
loss, which takes readers from the war-torn streets of Nazi-
occupied Athens through the military junta years and on into
the troubled city of recent times – and shows what happens
when ideology threatens to subsume our sense of humanity.

How To Be A Bad Birdwatcher
Simon Barnes

ISBN 9781780710470   Paperback £8.99

"Barnes is a unique voice, always willing to challenge conventional wisdom and look for deeper meanings..."
Sunday Telegraph

Birdsong is not just about natural history. It is also about our history. We got melody from the birds as we got rhythm from the womb.

This vital book – with a free podcast – takes you from winter into deepest spring, teaching you to how recognise song after song as the chorus swells. You start with robin, and end up listening to nightingales.

Along the way, you will learn something of the science of birdsong – the difference between song and call, the physiology of songbirds, what birdsong tells us about evolution, and indeed the very beginnings of life itself. The aim is to give you a flying start in birdsong so that, after reading this book, you'll be listening to order, not chaos, to Bach, not white noise. You will be more aware of the wild world, and better able to understand it.

The Social Animal
David Brooks

ISBN 9781780720371   Paperback £8.99

No. 1 International Bestseller

"Brooks gets inside the head, explains how the brain works... it's like frieze-framing a novel and discussing the motivation of the characters. It's fascinating..." *Evening Standard*

This is the happiest story you will ever read. It's about two people who led wonderfully fulfilling, successful lives.

The odd thing was, they weren't born geniuses. They had no extraordinary physical or mental gifts. Nobody would have picked them out at a young age and said they were destined for greatness.

How did they do it?

In case of difficulty in purchasing any Short Books
title through normal channels, please contact
BOOKPOST Tel: 01624 836000
Fax: 01624 837033
email: bookshop@enterprise.net
www.bookpost.co.uk
Please quote ref. 'Short Books'